Obesity

Laura Coe

A Philosophical Guide to
Lighten Your Life

EMOTIONAL OBESITY: A PHILOSOPHICAL
GUIDE TO LIGHTEN YOUR LIFE
ISBN 978-1-61961-307-2

This book is dedicated to the moment when the universe mirrored my dreams and I finally looked back and saw myself. The universe showed itself through many of you and for that I am eternally grateful.

For Jill Harris, my wife, my friend, and my spiritual classroom. Emotional Obesity is because of you and belongs to you; this is my version of a love letter.

For Nate Coe, my son, my heart, my spiritual teacher. You embody all that is right in the world and when I forget, your presence reminds me.

Contents

Acknowledgments

I would like to thank Christy Henry and Andrea Wishom for their early encouragement in writing this book and their enduring faith in my ability when I had none. Thank you to my long lost cousin Ron Lieber and his wife Jodi Kantor for introducing me to Tim Grahl and the world of self-publishing, without which this book might not have been written. I want to thank Ryan Holiday for his guidance and for introducing me to his very talented circle. Which brings me to my savior—my editor, Ann Maynard at Command Z. Your personal dedication to excellence is rare, inspiring, and deeply appreciated. Jennifer Gessner, Michelle and Gar Taylor, Justin and Lindsey Richland, Fred and Christy Henry, Beth Richie and Cathy Cohen, Ale and Tom Linquist, Brock and Liz Haldeman, Natalie Tessler and Ricky Ginsberg, Ted Gonder and Franzi Becker, and Lynn Auerbach, I thank you for your love and support as I stumbled through my mid-life crisis to find my passion. And a special thank you to my brother and his family: Brian, Tracy, Lilly, and Jason. Brian, my life coach, best friend, and brother, thank you for being you; if we cycle through lives, you have lived many because your wisdom is otherworldly. Special thanks to Lilly for her weekly comments on my blog; the best I received. I want to thank my parents, Fredric and Eleanor Coe, for coming along on this journey despite how foreign it may have seemed, and for loving me anyway. And finally, I want to thank a small piece of stone outside of the University of Chicago Medical Center. Although my father tripped on you and broke his kneecap, it allowed us to repair our relationship in ways I never believed possible. I have always known of his brilliance in the world, but, in my eyes, he was just my father. It has been a privilege to know the whole man. As we sat by the fire and read draft after draft of *Emotional Obesity*, my confidence as a writer came alive because of our time that winter. Thank you.

Introduction

This book is about how to design a life that makes *you* happy. If you have ever struggled with life choices that might offer success and fulfillment, that make you feel that sense of peace that we all long for, then this book will serve as a guide.

While we look to relieve our individual suffering in many ways, ancient wisdom speaks directly to our needs. While we attempt to feel better by accumulating more—seeking relief in external things, relationships, or substances—the answer we seek is within us at all times. Everything that we wish to experience, a sense of calm, joy, and abundance, rests within.

I discovered these teachings early in my life as a student in philosophy. Each time they spoke directly to my soul, yet what I knew to be a wealth of information left me bankrupt in execution. How do you design the life you desire? Simple: believe in your inner wisdom as your guide. Whatever creates a sense of enthusiasm is your personal Sherpa through this journey we call life. Unfortunately, most of us do not have the faith to follow.

Why?

Emotional weight. We are lied to as children. We are taught to turn off our inner wisdom. The artist becomes a lawyer, the athlete a doctor, and the teacher a corporate citizen. With each step away from our true path, a layer of emotional weight accumulates over our authentic voice leaving emotional illness: anger, shame, self-loathing, guilt, blame, and fear. It feels heavy. And if left unattended, it will become so much worse.

Surrender. We must follow, not lead, to find our fullest life. The mind wants to lead, but it is the interpreter of the soul. The mind is our tool belt equipped with language, knowledge, logic and many other useful skills to navigate our journey. However, it is not equipped with our truth. Truth only comes from our deeper, authentic self. To uncover the authentic self from beneath layers of emotional weight is not easy, but is the most worthwhile exercise to live a full life.

Fearlessness. We do not uncover our authentic self because we live in fear. Fear of not being enough. Fear that our truth is wrong. Fear that the very people we love will reject us for following our truth. Fear that we will not succeed. Scarcity.

In my own journey, my emotional weight began early. My mind slowly took control over my authentic self. First, my joy of athletics was replaced with a sedentary life. Then, my calling towards philosophy and spirituality was replaced with entrepreneurship. While I buried my voice behind layers of emotional weight, I found what most people would consider tremendous success. I built and sold a company before the age of 35. I had a beautiful family and even taught yoga on the side. I was also waking up almost every night in a panic. While some parts were authentic and others were not, what mattered was that I could not tell the difference.

I knew something had to change, but I was terrified to walk away from everything I built and step into the unknown. One day I made a commitment to find my authentic self. I dove back into my 20-year passion of philosophy and reread everything from Plato, Kant, Sutras, to modern spiritual texts. What proved to be the hardest journey that I have embarked on, much like getting in shape after denying physical health for a prolonged time, became my salvation.

Deep within all of us lies a space. T.S. Eliot said: "the still point in the turning world." I cannot tell you where it is because it has no physical shape. I also cannot tell you what it sounds like because it has no voice. I can tell you that we all have it—a subtle sense—our personal guide. When the mind is quiet, this sense will offer you *your* simple truth. It is your choice if you listen. If you chose to, everything you need to know about how to navigate your life will become available.

This is what I call emotional fitness. You may not sweat, lose weight, or gain muscles, but you will feel better than ever. As you surrender to the truth of your life, and follow the will of the universe, layer after layer of weight will fall off, leaving you lighter and deeply fulfilled in every moment.

Part One

Emotional **Obesity**

द्रष्टृदृश्ययोः संयोगो हेयहेतुः ॥१७॥

The cause of suffering is the false union of the seer (purusha) and the seen (prakriti)

SUTRA 2.17

I made the decision to leave my job of 15 years at 30,000 feet in the air. Brian—my business partner, brother, and best friend—and I were on a plane home from a business trip in Denver and I was in tears. Again. Brian calmly sat next to me as we reviewed the well-worn list of pros and cons of leaving my job, just as we had done 100 other times that week. The list was so rehearsed that nothing new ever got discovered, but the process had become a daily ritual. Brian always had a very calming effect on me and patiently listened as I reviewed my life again.

The argument with myself went something like this:
I want the company to succeed.
I feel responsible.

I cannot do this forever.
Who gives up a well paying job?
I need a plan.
I never get to see my son.
I hate that the nanny is raising him.
I love working with Brian.
I never wanted to be a businessperson.

When I came to the end of my speech about all the complexities of my choice, I looked at my brother, waiting for him to affirm me: "Yes, Laura, this is the hardest decision facing mankind." He never went that far, but Brian usually would indulge my need to weigh the benefits and drawbacks of each side of the equation. This time, he simply looked at me and said, "You know, you can just quit. You don't have to work here anymore. The world's a big place."

In that moment it felt like someone had taken a four hundred pound weight off my chest. Tears rolled down my face as I made peace with my decision to leave the only job I ever had and the company I built from the ground up with my family.

Not only did I decide to leave my job, but I also wanted to move in a new direction. I wanted to pursue a path that honored my self, to incorporate the ideas I had learned as a philosophy student and dedicated yoga practitioner. I had spent 25 years reading everything from Plato to Kant to the Bhagavad Gita but did very little to actually apply what I had learned to my own life.

As I began to wrap my head around my decision, my mind wandered back to a sutra I had read and committed to memory years before: *The cause of suffering is the false union of the seer and the seen.* All this time I thought the answer to finding what I wanted was "out there," but now these 1700-year-old words were reverberating a different message through my core. My tears, my anxiety, my wasted time and energy were the outcome of years in which my focus had drifted away from the intelligence of my deeper instincts. Now these words were sinking into me in a way they never had before. *My truth is within me.* In that moment I felt calmer, stabilized by the ancient wisdom I had so dutifully studied.

I dedicated my transition process to finding more authenticity in my life as I had read about in these cherished texts. And for the first time in a long time, it felt truly possible.

After all, I had just spent the last hour bawling on an airplane—things could only improve from there.

Passion Six Feet Under

Americans can have it all. True, but what that means and how to get it all differs from person to person as much as snowflakes differ from flake to flake. Yet, the dream, the pursuit of happiness, is sold as one idea: house, marriage, kids, a Labrador, and a job that you enjoy enough to support it all.

I followed the prescription and checked off the boxes as if the American Dream were a to-do list.

One day I pulled up to my 1920's colonial home. I parked across the street and stared at the beautiful house with a deep sense of curiosity. *Whose house is this? Whose life is this?* Everything was exactly as I had made it and yet I did not feel connected to it. The home was beautiful. The chocolate Labrador was handsome and nice, as a Labrador should be. My son was healthy and happy. My relationship was challenging and great, as a relationship would be after 14 years. So with all this in place, why wasn't I happy? Why did I have a nagging sense that I needed more? What more could there even be?

I have always been fascinated with the idea of change. How we change as a result of our actions and how change affects our identity; what changes are true to the development of our selves, and what changes are not. I studied philosophy in college and even went on to graduate school with the goal of perhaps teaching philosophy one day. Then I went into business instead. I wanted to make changes to my life—to make it more authentic—and, to do so, I had to sort out the parts of myself that are changeable and the parts that are not: philosopher, mom, entrepreneur, wife, daughter, athlete, city-dweller, latte-lover, writer. All of the labels had piled up over time and I could no longer sort out what felt authentic to me and what didn't.

At 24, I started a company with my brother and father. It seemed like the "smartest" move I could make as a post-grad—and that presumption was publically affirmed less than ten years later. When I was 35, we sold the business to a Fortune 500 and I was offered an executive position that promised financial freedom for the rest of my life. All of the practical aspects of my life were well taken care of and that made it very difficult to admit that I was on the verge of daily panic attacks. Everyone who was looking from the outside in would think everything perfect, when in fact I had checked off all the boxes without feeling any of the fulfillment I desired.

Every evening I would go to sleep with anxiety and wake up in the middle of the night as if someone were holding my head underwater. I knew I had to get out of this situation, but to where? I had been working outside of my passions for so long that I forgot how to access my dreams, personal goals, and a sense of authenticity.

Two years of night sweats and constant panic all came to a

head on that flight home from Denver. I sat back in my American Airlines seat, took a deep breath, and decided to start incorporating my favorite pearls of wisdom into my current life struggles. I began with something I never thought I would do, but had read about for years. I set an intention. I thought, "I would love to quit my job before the end of the summer so that I could transition my son into school." He was starting nursery school in the fall and our nanny of nearly three years was moving. It was only May so I had a few months to figure out a transition that would work for everyone. "Yes," I breathed again, "I will find a way out before September."

The Universe Spoke

"And, when you want something, all the universe conspires in helping you to achieve it."

— PAULO COELHO, THE ALCHEMIST

When you want something, you must work harder, longer, faster in order to achieve it. This was a lesson I, and so many others, have received throughout our lives. In fact, I had lived practically my entire life by the idea that the path to success required me to bust my ass and grind toward my goals. I believed my future was under my control, and surrendering that control was unthinkable. Now my thinking was starting to change.

The Alchemist, by Paulo Coelho, sold 65 million copies because its simple lessons for the main character, Santiago, are lessons for the ages *from* the ages. It's also a great story.

But one element of Coelho's narrative made me bristle: the idea that "the universe" can help you achieve what you want.

I was resistant to the idea because it flew in the face of everything I had believed for so long. It also rustled up my pride. I believed that if I worked hard enough, I could achieve my goals without help; and even worse, I believed that if I *did* seek and accept help from someone else it would somehow lessen my personal achievement. And if I sought help from "the universe"? Well, that would probably make me some kind of new age hippie.

As much as I fought off the idea, I couldn't get it out of my mind—especially as the clock ticked down toward my September deadline. Weeks had passed since my tearful declaration, and I hadn't made a single move toward it. I was frustrated with myself. I was also afraid and didn't really know what to do. The combination of fear, frustration, confusion, and desire was potent (and really uncomfortable). It started to make me consider ideas that I would have never entertained, including the idea of a helpful universe. After all, I had exhausted all the avenues I knew and was ready to open myself to something new—I was desperate! So I decided I was willing to try out this insane, silly, ridiculous notion that the universe was on my side and would work with me. Then the funniest thing happened: it worked.

"We got our number."

"Already? It's only July."

The company that acquired us had two seasons: hiring and firing. We hired in the winter, held headcounts in the spring, and then the dreaded *number* would come in the late summer. It was the amount of money we had to reduce from our spending so the company could hit its budget and the stock price would not be hurt. Brian had called me with the news.

"What is it?" I asked, as my breath tightened.

"$350,000."

"Ouch," I said, "and I'm assuming they want it in head-counts?" The board always wanted the reduction covered by headcounts—also known as "firing people for no reason."

"You can put yourself on the list and go," Brian replied. "It would also save a lot of other people from losing their jobs. The only problem is that I need an answer by the end of the weekend."

I had 48 hours to decide.

In the eight weeks since my mid-air decision to leave the only career I'd ever known, I had successfully avoided for-mulating my exit strategy by getting back to work. As the weeks went by, I would find myself revisiting the question of leaving my job and doubting my decision. I had no idea what I was going to do. I felt lost. I felt scared. I started to think of reasons to stay through the end of the year ("Yes, that might be smarter"), and then I would interrupt myself mid-thought with the reminder that I had made my decision and that I had to stand by it. Then I would think, "I release control and I will find a way to make this happen".

Now that it *was* happening, I returned to my list. It was the weekend. The clock was ticking, a 48-hour countdown. In my head the voices were screaming:

I cannot leave.

I have to keep my job.

What am I going to do all day?

I am going to be so bored.

I went from $15,000 a year to an executive salary and stock options.

Who leaves that?
My parents will never understand or support this decision.
There is something else out there for me.
What if I am wrong and this decision destroys everything I have worked so hard for?

To manage my anxiety (or so I thought), I was calling my well-worn list of supporters to rehearse the pros and cons of my departure over and over and over. I believed it was helping quell my internal battle, yet with every rehearsal and repetition, the weight of the decision became increasingly magnified. In a moment of indecision vertigo, I came back to reality, threw my phone down, and sat with my truth.

24 hours later I came out triumphant. I remembered my intention, that this was what I truly wanted. Yes, I had a lot to lose—I'd staked my entire identity (and salary) on my career as a high-powered female executive—and I had no idea what I was stepping into. But, I remembered the peace that I felt that day on the plane when I set the intention to leave my job and be home with my son. I never planned to be at the company forever. If I couldn't bring myself to leave now, when would I? "Funny," I thought, "my experiment of setting an intention, letting go and allowing the opportunity to present itself actually worked."

I called Brian. "Put me on the list—I am going to do it."

"Are you sure?" he asked. "They'll make an announcement to all the employees and executives. The turnaround will be quick."

"Yup," I said, "Put me on the list. I am ready to go."

And, that was it. In a sentence, I changed my life's course.

The announcement went out. Many conversations ensued, filled with tears, shock, and gratitude. There was the goodbye party, speeches, toasts, and good wishes. Then, in a moment, my office was empty. My email went blank and my calendar was clear. Everything that filled the days and nights of my life—that had for so long seemed so pressing and urgent—was gone in seconds.

I woke up the next morning without a Blackberry blinking red with hundreds of unread emails; there was just an ad from Gap and a few notes congratulating me on my new life. For the first time since my son was born, I was alone with him for an entire day with no distractions. We went to the Shed Aquarium in Chicago. We did not rush because I had nowhere else to be. We made our way over to our favorite lunch spot, Le Colonial, for a date. I sipped my cup of green tea and watched him try to lift the toy whale we just purchased into a cup of water with his chopsticks and I was truly happy. I was happy in a way that I had not experienced in a long, long time.

It was impossible for me to doubt the obviousness of the choice presented to me. It truly seemed that something outside of myself, the universe perhaps, had pulled some strings to point me down this new path—"conspiring" to make things happen, as Paulo Coelho might say. It certainly felt that way at least. I no longer felt like I was swimming upstream. In fact, it felt easy. I realized that "trusting the universe" is not about believing in the mystical, it is about understanding that my timing and the world's may not always sync up. It's about understanding that sometimes "grinding toward a goal" is really just spinning your wheels.

When I chose to leave my company, I made the decision to leave my past. Now I was starting my future. This was the beginning of a new journey in search of myself, a journey to find the person I abandoned long ago.

It's You

Three years later, on a random Tuesday night and in the company of new friends, my life took another big turn. Glasses of Malbec in hand, Justin, Lindsey, Jill and I seized the opportunity to get to know each other a bit better while our kids played underfoot. In one of those moments that I had come to dread since I left my job, the conversation turned to me. "What do you do for a living?"

What seemed like a simple conversation starter was actually a portal into my midlife crisis.

My efforts towards a still-unrealized new career were masking an internal struggle about which I had no awareness of. There had been plenty of options, sure, but the career choices I made had never felt like they were my own. To compensate, I had a carefully crafted (and completely inauthentic) response.

"I worked with my family to create a health care company that builds programs for people with chronic illnesses." My job, I would always continue to tell them, "was to build systems using information technology, branding, and best practices to help patients with kidney stones get access to the preventative treatments developed by my father. Over 15 years my brother and I built a company that took our father's life work out to patients nationwide."

I continued to tell them that when we sold the company, I left to be home with my three-year-old son, ease the working mom guilt and find a career that felt more in line with my passions. *There, I said it,* I would think. Then, I would try to change the subject while a wave of emptiness coursed through me.

I had worked hard and I hoped that the person asking would be impressed by my past achievements because it would help me feel as though I had made the right decision to have spent 15 years in a career that I never felt connected to. You would think that I would have learned after the first 100 times that the validation I was seeking was hard to come by.

Justin and Lindsey did not oblige me with a subject change.

"So what are you doing now?"

I explained that I wanted to do something more "authentic", a word that had become my worst nightmare. *Be authentic! How hard could that be?* I explained that I had considered a wide variety of possibilities: opening a yoga studio, running a wellness center, a bakery, a waxing chain, working as a therapist or life coach, and now, the latest, becoming an author.

Did I mention I was having a midlife crisis?

The honest answer was, I was trying to find my true self and it was much harder than I expected. Although I was proud of the success of our company, I never felt that I was doing what I was meant to do. When I left my job, I had one goal: do something that felt entirely authentic. I wanted to be the person who loved what she did. I wanted the feeling that I was doing what I was meant to do. But even with the best of intentions, my goal of living from my authentic self was proving totally unsuccessful.

The weight that had lifted off of me when I decided to leave my old job was a short-lived relief. As each failed attempt to find an authentic career ensued, I felt the weight pile back on. These days, my emotional life felt heavier than ever and my true self—which I knew was still there—felt buried beneath layer after layer of unresolved issues: anxiety, fear, pain, judgment, and self-doubt. I felt incapacitated by it, held back, and I had no idea how to get rid of it.

The idea of emotional weight (and emotional fitness) was one I had already been playing with for a while. I realized that in many ways our emotional health operates like our physical health: we can "feed" ourselves in a healthy way and develop regular routines to strengthen our emotional lives, or, if left neglected, our emotional issues could build up and have a detrimental impact on our lives. I called my idea Emotional Obesity.

Emotional Obesity was the book that I wanted to write and had been working toward, on and off, but had recently given up on completely. A writer himself, Justin, ignored my long list of failed career dabbles and perked up when I mentioned my attempt at authorship. "What are you writing?" I wasn't too happy to recount yet another failed attempt to find my life's passion manifest through my career. But his interest inspired me and I sheepishly began explaining.

"We need daily habits," I said, "to maintain healthy internal lives just as we need habits pertaining to what we eat and how we take care of our bodies to maintain good physical health."

As I talked about emotional weight and its ability to direct our choices and actions away from the desires of our true selves, Justin stared at me intensely. *Too intensely.*

"Okay, what?" I finally asked.

Justin smiled and peered over his glasses at me. "You are the book and the book is you."

I stopped. This was one of those moments when time slows and everything goes quiet because your whole being knows that something important is happening and you need to pay attention.

"What?" I uttered. (It was the only response I could muster).

"You took off three years to find your true self while trying to write a book about how our true selves are buried under emotional weight. You are the book and the book is you."

He was right. In my quest to create an authentic life I had allowed my choices and actions to be guided by the same voices and beliefs that I was trying to avoid. I had freed myself from a career I never wanted but never set down the burden of my emotional weight. All of the layers—the negative emotions, learned values, self-imposed limitations, and judgments—that I thought I had "gotten over" were still there, wrapped around my spirit and muting its voice. I was the book and the book was me.

I was emotionally obese.

What Is Emotional Obesity?

Emotional Obesity is a barrier around our soul. All the negative ideas and thoughts we have collected throughout our lives exist as layered weight around our true spirit. That spirit, in its perfect form, is completely unaffected but it is muted, unable to be heard underneath blanket after blanket, layer after layer of our emotional weight. **Our negative thoughts will stay exactly where they are as long as we avoid them—an infinitely more comfortable option—just as the unhealthy fat on our bodies will linger if we avoid physical activity in favor of the couch.**

In both cases, we will carry that weight until we decide to make a change.

Fortunately, just as it is possible to improve our physical health with nutrition and fitness, we can improve our emotional health in a very similar way. By learning to manage the messages we tell ourselves, we can ensure that the things we feed our mind and spirit are positive for our wellbeing—

emotional nutrition, if you will—rather than defaulting to negative emotions (a.k.a. emotional junk food) that offer no benefit. We can improve our emotional fitness with actual exercises that strengthen our emotional lives and help replace bad habits with good ones. As we rid ourselves of the negative messages we carry around—as we lose emotional weight—the barriers around our soul drop off and the voice of our spirit can be heard in its full beauty.

My own journey toward getting in emotional shape didn't start with a bang; it was more like a quick fizzle. I realized that I had no idea how to even start managing the messages of my mind. It felt like I had come home with a new pair of running shoes but had no idea what to do with them. So I sat back down on the couch.

My first inclination was to silence my mind or at least try really hard to ignore it. That seems natural, right? Move forward, move on, don't stop and don't look. It was a response I was conditioned for. It was familiar and comfortable. On the other hand, my emotions could hurt, they could certainly be uncomfortable, and at times I thought they might consume me. What would I do with them anyway? Without tools, techniques or support, looking too closely at my emotional world only left me feeling worse. Why engage with emotions that only make me feel bad? I thought stepping over my emotions gave me the strength to continue my job search, and I kept thinking this way until, after getting lost in an endless cycle, I decided to question my process.

As I struggled, I realized that improving my emotional health had a major challenge that I never had to face in my efforts to stay in good physical shape: Addressing the state of my emotional health felt like a personal attack. It felt like I was saying there was something wrong with *me*. Taking stock of my emotions caused more pain and made me feel defensive and ashamed. It became apparent that I would never be able to pursue emotional fitness while taking the process personally. The first thing I had to change was the mindset with which I approached my emotional life.

And I would do this by using the texts that inspired me and countless others seeking answers for thousands of years. Surely, the ideas hold value for solving this modern-day issue. Each time I turned to the ancient wisdom for solutions, I found exactly what I needed: advice that holds up over the ages and makes perfect sense for my personal goals. The only challenge was figuring out how to make these ideas practical every day solutions.

The rest of this book is an effort to explain what I found when I peeled back the layers of weight that had piled on over the years and how kept the weight off. With each step, I learned what stood in the way of my ability to feel lighter in my life.

1. Culture: The perspectives in our collective culture that make getting in emotional shape challenging.
2. Impostor Voices (i.e. my mind): I relied on my mind for guidance but discovered it was my biggest obstacle to losing emotional weight. So many of our thoughts are shaped by external forces and can't be trusted.
3. My Authentic Voice: What is this mysterious place? It is not a voice; it is a sensation that needs a voice and is the guiding principle of a happy life design.
4. Emotional Weight Loss is Not New: The ancients already knew the value of emotional fitness.

5. Junk Food Thoughts: When we eat a diet of junk food thoughts we suffer from their unhealthy effects, just like our bodies suffer from junk food.

6. Storytelling: Our lives are subjective realities, so it's important to tell a good story about your life.

7. Emotional Nutrition: Feed yourself thoughts that nourish your mind just as you eat foods that nourish your body and you can have the life you desire.

8. Emotional Workouts: Years of unhealthy thoughts have a negative impact on our wellbeing through anger, resentments, self-neglect, blame, shame, and fear. Working out and staying emotionally fit is the most effective way to avoid the impact of these negative emotions.

9. Maintaining Emotional Health: Locating your authentic self is half the battle. The ability to return to this place for guidance is the key ingredient to ongoing emotional health.

10. The Secret to Long-Term Success: Habit, action, faith, and surrender.

A Change in Mindset

"Stop acting so small. You are the universe in ecstatic motion."

— RUMI

Emotional fitness is challenging because we take it personally; the need for change feels like criticism because the implication is that we are not good enough the way we are, so we are quick to defend ourselves. It is a far cry from the objective way we deal with our physical health. When someone learns that they need surgery, they may respond with fear, anxiety or sadness; and that's all understandable—it is not good news. But, I could never imagine anyone saying, "How could that doctor say that to me? I am a good person and I am offended that he thinks the mole on my back needs to be taken off!"

We don't take our physical health issues as a personal affront, yet our emotional needs (or the emotional needs of others) can immediately put us on the defensive, or shut us down. If we are accused of anything—anger, resentment, jealousy, or feeling victimized—we feel attacked and respond accordingly.

Why not accept that part of being alive is to struggle with unwanted feelings, and that it is okay to be jealous, angry, or resentful? Let's choose to take the same stance with emotional issues that we take with physical issues: **To be human is to have negative emotions; just as to be human is to have problems with our bodies.** Our emotional health is not a criticism—or even an indication—of who we are. We are not our negative emotional states just as we are not our illnesses. To improve upon our emotional lives, makes us happier, it does not change who we are.

Our emotional life is complex and dynamic. We cannot be cheery all the time and to expect otherwise is unrealistic. We do not live in a state of cheeriness; we live in a place of contentment. As we experience moments of joy like seeing a goofy puppy, earning a promotion, enjoying a hug, a vacation, a sunset or a positive thought, we feel cheer. It is a fleeting state, however, and will not last without another moment to prolong it. **Cheeriness cannot be our default state because our emotions are not static.** Accepting that fact is critical to our emotional wellbeing and, once we do so, we can use our fluctuating emotions to our advantage.

After all, our emotions are telling us something and judging them, ignoring them, or pushing them down will guarantee that we don't get the valuable message they are relaying to us. Curiosity about our emotional world is the antidote to shame and judgment. Moments of pain, anger, frustration, sadness, boredom, or any other "unwanted" emotion are actually opportunities to investigate negative feelings.

From there, we can discern what they are telling us and begin to understand our real needs and desires.

Our bodies send us physical messages all the time. Dry skin tells me I need to drink water; a stomachache suggests I did not eat well. Our bodies tell us when we've put something bad into them (or if we are withholding something good) and incentivize us to investigate the cause of our discomfort and to avoid it in the future. Our emotional reactions work the same way. They help us understand our desires, dislikes, or even our fears. Positive emotional reactions tell us what activities and environments make use come alive: *This feels great! Keep it up!* Negative emotional reactions dull our life force: *This is bad for me*, or, *I'm not getting something I need.* Choosing curiosity over judgment allows us to investigate what that message is (and whether it is something to seek or avoid in the future).

Rather than denying the origins of your emotional reactions, instead ask yourself why you are angry, defensive or sad. *Why was I upset with a friend? What is that bringing up in me?* Remind yourself that there is nothing there to judge as right or wrong. It is an opportunity to learn about your needs or to grow. *Maybe my reaction is telling me that I need something. Maybe this friend is not meeting my needs and our friendship is not right for me.*

When we judge ourselves for feeling bad, we cheat ourselves out of the chance to grow and evolve our lives. Ignoring or "stuffing" our negative emotions down will only add to our emotional weight. **Curiosity allows us to figure out what is making us feel bad and learn to avoid it in the future, just as we would avoid something that gave us a stomachache.** Changing our mindset starts with accepting our emotional life in all its forms—good, bad, and ugly crying on the floor—just as we accept that our bodies will break down sometimes. It's not personal; it's just human. Every overflow of emotion has a message, a truth about your self, if you choose to look for it. Making the choice to change your perspective on your emotional health is the first thing you can do to start embracing it.

Rumi, a 13th century poet, understood the idea that we needed to change our mindset to feel better. He tells us to "stop acting so small," that we are more than our flaws, our missteps, and our petty emotional states. We are "the universe in ecstatic motion." As far as mindset changes go, I can't think of anything bigger or more effective. We cannot take the details of our lives so seriously. We are more than the details that we feel so ashamed by—we are the universe!

We Are Battling a Cultural Mindset

As a culture, we have embraced the value of physical fitness. Over the last several decades we have made workouts, doctor appointments and healthy eating an expected part of our daily lives. What if we had the same cultural view about emotional wellness? How would we benefit from a culture that prioritized emotional wellness?

As a society, we have not embraced emotional care as a normal part of our everyday lives. We all participate in routines and systems that care for our physical health: we shower, brush our teeth, put on lotion, and dress according to the standards of our jobs or daily routines. Some may try to eat a healthier breakfast, exercise, or go to a physician for a preventative checkup. These routines are not just culturally accepted; they're often socially mandated. Still, for all the billion dollar industries—from healthcare to makeup to green juice—little attention and value are given to maintaining our emotional wellbeing.

Not only do we have few routines for our emotional health, we do not ever talk about it. I could tell my friend that I spent the day getting my haircut at a high-end salon, detailing my choice between highlights and lowlights before talking about shopping for clothes and I would find perfect social acceptance. However, if I say that I am spending the day working on maintaining my emotional state, I would be met with concern and potential rejection. "What is wrong? Is there a crisis?" Without a traumatic reason, working on our inner life sounds strange. And because it might sound strange, no one talks about it.

Imagine inviting me to a dinner party with a group of your friends. When the moment arises, I explain my day: I ate some sushi, had an amazing almond milk latte, went to yoga, got groceries at Whole Foods, and went to the doctor for a check up. This kind of conversation is perfectly acceptable to a group that has never met me. Now, what would the response be if I said, "I woke up this morning feeling unworthy, but I took a few minutes to meditate on my feelings and was able to turn my day around"?

Can you imagine how faces would drop? The silence that would ensue?

The judgment that would follow for divulging a weakness would be palpable. And, later, imagine the phone calls recapping the evening's discomfort from my expression of honest emotion. Yet, at the same dinner party with the same friends, I could admit to any of my physical flaws without consequence. I could talk about how unhappy I am with my body, with my job, my relationship or my family. Why would there be so much shame in the admission of a flaw in my emotional state of being?

How can we get in shape emotionally when we are too ashamed to admit our imperfections? We work to conceal our flaws for fear that if our humanity—which consists of good and bad qualities—shows, people will see that we are not perfect. Then what? We are not lovable? We are not good enough? We are convinced that to be honest and vulnerable in our truth will result in the loss of those dearest to us. We think no one wants to see us in our entirety because we were taught to hide our emotional imperfections or to move past them—they are seen as a weakness, not a fact of life.

We do not have systems to measure emotional fitness because we are not willing to admit there is something to build a system around. We live in a culture of emotional shame; it teaches us to be tough and to keep our problems to ourselves. We believe we are exposing the core of ourselves by admitting what we think and feel. It's a scary thing. We fear that if others see the negative state of our emotional life, they will judge us. So, we push it out of our consciousness. Unfortunately, what we feel, though buried and not bothering anyone, can have an enormous impact on our lives.

And *still*, fitting into cultural norms at the expense of our emotional health, feels like the safer option. It's time to change that.

In order to fit into (and thereby perpetuate) cultural norms, we buy into perfectly acceptable reasons for avoiding our internal lives. In order to lead an emotionally healthy life, we must reframe our individual perspectives to go against established cultural norms like the following:

CULTURAL NORM #1: "GETTING OVER IT" IS THE STRONGER CHOICE.

Feeling bad is weak. When faced with feelings of shame, guilt, and unworthiness the strongest thing we can do is move past it.

NEW PERSPECTIVE #1: FACING YOUR UNWANTED FEELINGS IS THE STRONGER CHOICE.

All we're really doing when we "get over" our feelings is pushing them away from consciousness, instead of dealing with them and their sources. In doing so we build a stockpile of our issues, adding more and more until they become a tremendous weight we carry around unknowingly. This weight can keep us from living our fullest life. The braver decision is to face them head on, determine where they are coming from, and deal with them directly.

CULTURAL NORM #2: TALKING ABOUT YOUR EMOTIONAL HEALTH IS SOCIALLY AWKWARD.

When your mind is telling you, "I just don't think I deserve love," or, "I am not worthy of the things that I want," you need to keep it to yourself. You will make other people feel awkward or they might judge you for your flaws. Nobody wants to hear about that. That's too much information (TMI).

NEW PERSPECTIVE #2: TALKING ABOUT YOUR EMOTIONAL HEALTH IS HEALTHY.

You are actively working to keep yourself—your ENTIRE self—healthy. And that is something to be proud of. And talking about your emotions does not mean you are not a good listener or that you are self-absorbed. When something in life is not working, you want to find solutions. If you ignore your emotional challenges, you will not overcome them.

CULTURAL NORM #3: DON'T LET YOUR HUMANITY SHOW.

Everyone has issues and you're no different, but that's not what people want to see. It is better to look like you've got everything together.

NEW PERSPECTIVE #3: LET YOUR HUMANITY SHOW.

Everyone has issues and you're no different. We're all fighting against our own fears and anxieties because we're all human. By being honest with others about what you're going through, you will allow yourself to be supported instead of isolated. Once supported you can heal yourself and ultimately pay it forward by supporting those you care about. If everyone hides his or her truth and remains in pain, then no one can truly support anyone. The cycle will just continue. Like group workouts, jogging, gyms, and yoga classes, working with others can give the needed support to help overcome those unwanted emotions.

The fact is the longstanding cultural norms pertaining to our emotional health are not good for us. When we feel shame about our emotional flaws, whether it comes from our selves or our culture (or likely combination of both), we are far less likely to view them as something we can change. Instead, we feel like they need to be hidden. So we carry our emotional weight with us, allow it to direct our choices and actions, and we move further and further away from our true selves. We become emotionally obese.

What Does Emotional Obesity Look Like?

How can we know if we are emotionally obese when we do not have a scale or a doctor to tell us so? Without objective measures we have to rely on ourselves to diagnose the extent of our emotional weight and the impact it is having on our health. What does Emotional Obesity look like?

Symptoms may include: an unhappy relationship, not feeling content, feeling stuck in the wrong job, or with the wrong friends; to live regularly in fear, anger, frustration, depression, or any other negative thoughts. These are the signs of Emotional Obesity.

Perhaps you believe that safety comes with a certain amount of money. You fear the idea of living without enough so every choice you make is made with consideration to your finances. You work 80-hour weeks or are constantly striving for a higher-paying job. It's a miserable grind but the thought of leaving is terrifying.

Maybe your life feels like a continual cycle of disappointments. Your expectation is that everything you embark on will not live up to your hopes or dreams, so why bother dreaming and why bother trying? Nothing will turn out well anyway. Life is disappointing and having hope or faith that things will go well is simply naïve. It is better to stay where you are than to be let down again.

Perhaps, you feel like you're not deserving of the good things in your life. You feel like you're not a good person and do not deserve the things that you desire. The opportunity to follow one's passion is reserved for those who have earned it and you have no such expectation for yourself.

All of these are signs of Emotional Obesity. **When our sense of self comes from a negative place and our actions are dictated from that place, we are emotionally obese.**

We believe we "push through" negative experiences and thoughts, when all we're really doing is avoiding their existence. But we cannot escape their influence. As we make daily choices about everything from dinner plans to relationships to career moves, those feelings guide our decisions. These unresolved issues create imposter voices, negative patterns of thought that we mistake for our true selves. We are easily tricked by these impostor voices until we learn how to spot them. Without awareness of the source of our thoughts, our choices are not reflective of our real desires. We move further and further from the life we truly want to live, which results in pain and suffering.

This was a lesson I had to learn the hard way.

Impostors

Egoism is the identification, as it were, of the power of the Seer (purusha) with that of the instrument of seeing.

— SUTRA 2.6

Taking action is easy. Determining the origin of the action you choose is the tricky part.

I read and reread the sutras over and over and over, staring at them, knowing that they were saying something of value. I could not understand how these thousand-year-old lessons applied to my own life, yet I felt the power of the message. The wisdom of the sutra urges us to question the origin of our thoughts. Our perception, our narrative, our senses—all of the tools we use to understand our world—misinform our decisions. The combination of perceiving the world with the critical step of asking how it feels within allows us to design a life we desire.

Urban Shanti was the name of the yoga studio I was going

to open. I loved practicing yoga and had earned my instructor certification years before. Better still, with one successful company already under my belt, I was confident that I could build another business from the ground up. It was an opportunity to leverage my skills and experience and apply them to something I truly enjoyed. And, after all, I left my old job to find something that I loved and that felt authentic. This seemed like a great solution.

When I left my company, my plan was simple. I would explore opportunities as they presented themselves and would remain very open to new directions. Before making a decision, I would look inward, tune into my internal voice, and assess how I truly felt about the opportunity. If something felt bad, then I would know that I was not doing the right thing. I assumed that as I explored different options, my internal voice would accurately steer me toward—or away from—particular paths until I landed exactly where I needed to be. **It never occurred to me to question whether my internal voice would mislead me.** Instead, I charged forward with Urban Shanti.

I convinced my good friend, Amy, to open the new studio with me and we set to work selecting a space and brainstorming potential workshops. We went to Michigan for a weekend with vision boards, our yoga mats, and plans for long meditations to help inspire us. After we finalized our vision, other friends offered the services of their design firm free of charge. We had a website, a logo, and even explored Urban Shanti t-shirts. We were having a great time planning and dreaming but, little by little, a sinking feeling set in as my internal voices—the ones I heard on the plane—started talking.

I am nearly 40—that's too old to teach yoga.

I don't know enough about workshops, incense and meditation pillows.

There is no money in yoga studios.

I can barely touch my toes.

I will not be home for my son again.

What am I doing?

Ultimately, the voices won out over my resolve and I allowed Urban Shanti to fall by the wayside. I was disappointed, of course, but I felt that it was the right decision. I believed that I was staying true to my authentic self. I trusted the voice in my head and allowed it to lead me in a different direction. And then I did it again. And again. And again.

For two years.

There was the integrative health center (*"Wow, there will be a lot of insurance bills to track."*), the bakery (*"You sure would have to get up early!"*), and the waxing studio (*"Waxing??"*). After passing on so many amazing opportunities, I was starting to question what was wrong with me. I believed that by listening to my authentic voice I would find the right path, but all it had really done was make me a really effective quitter. I had over-flexed this new muscle and, instead of feeling assured and confident, I found myself sore, tired, and confused.

How could this many jobs all be wrong?

You Cannot Always Trust Your Thoughts (Even When They Sound Like You)

When I am not speaking I can hear myself talk. In fact, I wish I would not have to hear myself as often as I do.

My thoughts sound exactly like me. The tone of the voice and the way that it speaks, from sentence structure to vocabulary, is indistinguishable from my own. This voice, the one that follows me everywhere I go, sounds exactly like me as I debate, discuss, ponder, worry, criticize, and dream inside my head.

I never thought that my internal voice couldn't be trusted. In fact, it never even occurred to me to ask that question. But after two years of following what I believed was my authentic voice, I realized I had been wrong.

Gratitude is one of my core values and my actions over the course of my job search—passing up countless opportunities, cashing in favors, and letting down my friends—flew directly in the face of it. That was wrong. **Your authentic voice will never contradict your value system.** I realized that the voice I had been listening to was from an outside source, an impostor.

The fact is, your voices are not entirely your own. Though it is certainly enlightening, it's a painful thing to realize that these impostors exist. Harder still, to realize that some of them aren't coming from you at all. Over the course of my search for an authentic career I had been listening to a long list of external voices; expectations, definitions, and ideas that I had held for so long without ever asking myself if I really believed them.

I was raised next door to University of Chicago. My father was world famous in his area of expertise and maintained a social circle of other academics and highly distinguished achievers. Naturally, I believed that everyone had a PhD, MBA, MD or some combination of letters after their name. Success, therefore, had a very narrow definition: it was fancy degrees and doing something "important". I never defined what "important" meant either—something between saving whales from extinction and curing cancer. So, when I attempted to create my new authentic career, I was unknowingly working those standards into the foundation for my decisions.

Then came the $50,000 question: Do I actually agree with that definition of success? My answer was a resounding "NO".

My definition of success was a learned value—one I didn't even agree with—and I had allowed that voice to direct the search for my life's new path. Armed with this new perspective, I re-examined my list of reasons for passing on Urban Shanti and I could immediately see its influence:

"A local, small business doesn't have national impact."

Without knowing it, I had measured my yoga studio against cancer cures, whale-saving, and brilliant inventions. I had even measured it against my old company. And when its impact potential fell short—which it obviously would—I understood that gap as a major strike against the idea. My external world had infiltrated my head.

I kept looking through my list. Were there any other statements that contradicted my actual beliefs? No question. I found two:

"I am nearly 40 — that's too old to teach yoga."

"I can barely touch my toes."

Somewhere I had picked up a clear concept of what a yoga instructor *should* look like and chose to believe that I wasn't cut out to teach because I didn't fit that mold. Never mind that my genetics-based lack of flexibility had never stood in the way of my personal yoga practice. Never mind that my age didn't prevent me from earning my certification (or that yoga instructors over 40 are awesome). I allowed the messages that I had picked up from my environment, media, and who-knows-where-else to dictate my thoughts and undermine my confidence in something I knew to be true.

I had never thought of myself as being particularly susceptible to these kinds of external ideas but, while I was not conscious of them, these voices were hard at work impacting my decisions while I believed them to be my authentic voice.

These internal impostors mixed seamlessly with my authentic internal voice but they shared one suspicious trait: They all came from negative places: judgment, fear, worry, anxiety, jealousy, and every other negative word that comes to mind. These voices were the product of my emotional weight. Sadly, I mistook them as my guiding, true voice and allowed them to lead me astray in my search for a new career.

Every option I considered was a business — something I had already been successful in — and this pleased those voices. The more my experience and expertise would contribute, the happier that voice became, and the further I would pursue that career path. After all, I wanted to find joy in my new job but I also wanted to be certain that I would be successful.

I now recognize my desire for certain success as a fear of failure. After all, if my new venture wasn't immediately successful, wouldn't that mean I had made the wrong choice? Wouldn't others shake their heads over my "fall"? Wouldn't that mean I wasn't as capable as I (or anyone else) thought? I could see my fear of failure written on my list:

"I don't know enough about workshops, incense and meditation pillows."

"There is no money in yoga studios."

I was afraid that I didn't know enough about yoga studios to make Urban Shanti a success. I was afraid that, even if the studio did well, I wouldn't be bringing home huge paychecks to signify that success which made me begin to judge myself from a place of "not good enough".

Your true voice will never come from a negative place and will never make you feel bad about yourself. **If your voice undermines your confidence, if it comes from fear, or if it is telling you that you are, "not good enough," it is an impostor**.

The problem with saying, "Don't trust the voices in your head," is that they're not all impostors. These voices are not always wrong. Your authentic voice is still speaking your truth and is just as easy to hear. It's just mixed in with the crowd.

My authentic voice was speaking along with the impostors when I was in doubt over whether to pursue Urban Shanti:

"I will not be home for my son again."

That was a true reason, a real value, that didn't fit with the yoga studio path. My authentic voice was telling me that Urban Shanti wasn't the right choice.

Listen to Your Gut

"Everything in the universe is within you. Ask all from yourself."

— RUMI

Despite the fact that the majority of the voices that steered me away from opening a yoga studio were impostors, I still knew that I made the right decision. And I knew it as soon as I made it.

I knew backing out was the right choice because I *felt better* once I did. This was how I knew I had tapped into the desires of my authentic self.

Rumi was right again. I had the answers I was seeking, but I was not practicing that in my life.

It wasn't the voices in my head that pushed me the hardest; it was the sinking feeling that accompanied them. Your true voice has something that your impostors don't: a good connection to your physical self. Listen to your gut. **If your**

body creates a sensation in opposition of your desire to move forward, listen to it.

Pressure in your head or chest, pain in your stomach, maybe tightness in your throat—whatever it is, it doesn't feel good.

Moving in a direction that honors your true self may create a sense of nervous excitement or challenge your commitment and dedication to your goal, but it will *feel* right, despite the potential challenges.

One of the first steps to emotional fitness is to understand that your voice, the one that sounds like you, can't always be trusted. Sometimes the voice will really come from your unique self and sometimes it is from an outside source, an impostor, but how do you know which is which? How do you test the validity of your voice?

How to Test the Validity of Your Voice

In a moment of negative emotional overwhelm, pause and ask yourself, "Where this is originating from?" Perform a scan of your brain and your body to assess whether you can trust your inner voice.

STEP ONE: BRAIN SCAN
Ask yourself:

- Am I blaming?
- Am I a victim?
- Am I coming from anger?
- Am I comparing?
- Do I want to be right?
- Is this the voice of "not good enough"?
- Is this the voice of low self-worth?
- Am I reacting to others' emotions and taking them on as my own?

STEP TWO: BODY SCAN

What is happening in your body? The symptoms of emotional Obesity can manifest themselves in your physical state. Scan your body and answer these questions:

- Do I feel pressure in my head?
- Are my eyes suddenly intense?
- Are my shoulders up to my ears?
- Is my throat tight or my mouth dry?
- How is my stomach? Is it feeling anxious or nervous?
- What about my chest? Is it tight? Does it have a sense of pressure?
- How about my heart? Is it feeling pain?

STEP THREE: ACCEPTANCE

If you answered yes to anything above, then your voice cannot be trusted to act in accordance with your higher self. Why? Because your body's intelligence is telling you that something is wrong. Just as an allergic reaction creates inflammation to warn us of potential harm, our minds and bodies are warning us of potentially harmful negative thoughts through physical discomfort. And, like we would want to avoid foods that create that negative physical outcome, we want to avoid thoughts that do, too.

Pain, whether it is emotional or physical, needs to be investigated. The tension in your body and the negative messages in your mind are the signs that your voice has been hijacked.

Do not take action if you suspect an impostor has taken charge.

My impostor voices—stemming from my fears, anxieties,

judgments, and learned values—were all emotional weight. And, as I could clearly see, they were weighing me down. I slowly became aware of the stories I was telling myself and began to question their validity. In other words, I was learning how to step onto the emotional scale and see how many emotional pounds I had gained.

THE EMOTIONAL SCALE

I have a confession: I hate scales. Who wants to weigh themselves? Because I hate them I try to avoid them but, let's be honest, there is inevitably a moment when my jeans no longer fit right and excuses like, "the dryer was too hot" no longer justify how tight the pants have really become.

The same is true on a personal level. I have an arsenal of excuses for why my life is not going exactly as I want but as with my ill-fitting jeans, there comes a moment when I have to get on the emotional scale.

STEP RIGHT UP

My life is comprised of all kinds of beliefs every day, week, and year. As I realized when I saw that my definition of success had been dictated by my upbringing, I had a lot of long-held beliefs that I had never taken the time to assess whether I truly believed them. By taking stock of what I actually believed, I started to understand what was important to me.

Take a moment and think about how much you value the beliefs listed below. Which are most important to you? It is okay if you are not practicing your beliefs—understanding them first is more important.

On a scale of one to ten, how would you rate the importance of these beliefs in your life?

"1" means this belief is not important.
"10" means it is critical to a well-lived life.

I believe that _____ is...

Personal Self Care	1 2 3 4 5 6 7 8 9 10
Being Compassionate	1 2 3 4 5 6 7 8 9 10
Practicing Gratitude Daily	1 2 3 4 5 6 7 8 9 10
Contributing to Society	1 2 3 4 5 6 7 8 9 10
Listening to Others	1 2 3 4 5 6 7 8 9 10
Outbursts of anger	1 2 3 4 5 6 7 8 9 10
Harboring Resentment	1 2 3 4 5 6 7 8 9 10
Controlling Others	1 2 3 4 5 6 7 8 9 10
Fearing Fear	1 2 3 4 5 6 7 8 9 10
Blaming Others or Myself	1 2 3 4 5 6 7 8 9 10
Shaming Others or Myself	1 2 3 4 5 6 7 8 9 10
Judgment	1 2 3 4 5 6 7 8 9 10
Denial as a Way to Cope	1 2 3 4 5 6 7 8 9 10
Faith	1 2 3 4 5 6 7 8 9 10
Surrendering	1 2 3 4 5 6 7 8 9 10
Letting go	1 2 3 4 5 6 7 8 9 10
Pushing back	1 2 3 4 5 6 7 8 9 10
Fighting to Get My Way	1 2 3 4 5 6 7 8 9 10
Communicating my Emotions	1 2 3 4 5 6 7 8 9 10
Being Vulnerable	1 2 3 4 5 6 7 8 9 10
Working Hard for What I Want	1 2 3 4 5 6 7 8 9 10
Family Time	1 2 3 4 5 6 7 8 9 10
Building Community	1 2 3 4 5 6 7 8 9 10
Celebrating Daily Success	1 2 3 4 5 6 7 8 9 10
Money Brings Safety	1 2 3 4 5 6 7 8 9 10
Success Brings Happiness	1 2 3 4 5 6 7 8 9 10

Okay, now let's go through the scale one more time. This time, rate **what you do** on a scale from 1–10.

"1" means you rarely take action.

"10" means you take massive action.

I take action towards...

Daily Self Care	1 2 3 4 5 6 7 8 9 10
Acting from Compassion	1 2 3 4 5 6 7 8 9 10
Practicing Gratitude Daily	1 2 3 4 5 6 7 8 9 10
Contributing to Society	1 2 3 4 5 6 7 8 9 10
Listening to Others	1 2 3 4 5 6 7 8 9 10
Outbursts of anger	1 2 3 4 5 6 7 8 9 10
Resentment as a part of life	1 2 3 4 5 6 7 8 9 10
Controlling Others	1 2 3 4 5 6 7 8 9 10
Fearing Fear	1 2 3 4 5 6 7 8 9 10
Blaming Others or Myself	1 2 3 4 5 6 7 8 9 10
Shaming Others or Myself	1 2 3 4 5 6 7 8 9 10
Judgment	1 2 3 4 5 6 7 8 9 10
Denial as a Way to Cope	1 2 3 4 5 6 7 8 9 10
Faith	1 2 3 4 5 6 7 8 9 10
Surrendering	1 2 3 4 5 6 7 8 9 10
Letting go	1 2 3 4 5 6 7 8 9 10
Pushing back	1 2 3 4 5 6 7 8 9 10
Fighting to Get My Way	1 2 3 4 5 6 7 8 9 10
Communicating my Emotions	1 2 3 4 5 6 7 8 9 10
Being Vulnerable	1 2 3 4 5 6 7 8 9 10
Working Hard for What I Want	1 2 3 4 5 6 7 8 9 10
Family Time	1 2 3 4 5 6 7 8 9 10
Building Community	1 2 3 4 5 6 7 8 9 10
Celebrating Daily Success	1 2 3 4 5 6 7 8 9 10
Money Brings Safety	1 2 3 4 5 6 7 8 9 10
Success Brings Happiness	1 2 3 4 5 6 7 8 9 10

Are there gaps between what you believe and what you do? There were certainly were for me.

My actions were not aligned with my true beliefs. I was not acting in accordance with my values. Since my actions are driven from my thoughts and beliefs, I have to make sure I am clear on what they are. If I am acting based on beliefs that are not mine, my life will be designed from outside my desires.

I believed in gratitude, but I was not practicing it daily.

I believed in compassion, but I was not as compassionate to others as I desired.

I believed in contributing to society, but I was only thinking about what I wanted in my career.

I do not believe in letting fear control my actions, but I allowed fear to do just that.

Every gap between my beliefs and my actions is emotional weight.

Your Emotional Weight is created by the actions you take that are not based on your beliefs.

For example:

If you believe that gratitude for life is important, how many times a day do you practice expressions of gratitude?

If you believe outbursts of anger are not beneficial, do you refrain from having outbursts?

How can our beliefs and actions be so misaligned?

I did not believe in outbursts of anger, yet that was not what I practiced. The reason was simple. When I felt confronted, I felt the person deserved my anger. In other words, I blamed the other person for behaving in a way that created my response. "I was only angry because *they* were confrontational."

No one can "make" you feel anything. Your actions are a choice. Every time you take action and it is not based on your beliefs, you are stepping in the wrong direction. Blaming others for your emotional state is easy. Taking responsibility for your own emotions is harder, but it is incredibly empowering. When you choose to act based on your true beliefs, you step towards your unique goals and dreams.

In reality, my choice to be angry is just that. My own choice. If someone is confrontational, then they are confrontational. I do not have to respond with anger, especially if I do not believe in anger as a way of conducting myself in life.

Is there a belief that you feel strongly about, but you do not practice?

Look back at the results of your emotional scale, select an area that has a sizeable gap between what you believe and what you do then do the following exercise:

Pick one belief this week. See how many times you can add it to your daily routine. Emotional fitness occurs when we strengthen the areas of our lives that are aligned with our desires. Lift an emotional weight and build muscle in an area that will better support your goals.

ONE MORE THING...

If you identify with the thoughts coming from just your senses without questioning how they feel, you will make a lot of choices and design a life from a place that lacks authenticity. I was searching for authenticity, but I could not start to find it because I did not understand this distinction.

What the Hell Is Authenticity Anyway?

"Authenticity...what the hell am I even looking for??" I asked myself this question so many times. On the surface it seemed like a fairly intuitive concept—"Be Authentic!"—but what did that actually feel like? Where was my authentic self and, more importantly, how would I know when I had found it?

The answer was: I needed to let it find me.

When it comes to tapping into your authentic self, there is no big "A-ha" moment in which you are washed over with a sense of Buddha-like calm, Ghandi-like wisdom, and brimming with self-assurance and readiness to proceed forward down an enlightened path. Nope. It's subtle. Like a beautiful sunset, or watching a smile creep over your baby's face as he nuzzles against you—you feel something inside you open. Time slows down and your mind quiets. Suddenly, somehow, the only thing in the world is what is directly in front of you. You feel full. Content. It is a feeling that is as much about recognition as it is about discovery.

I can't tell you what your authentic self looks like and feels like. You are unique, and what works for me may not work for you. To find what your authentic self feels like, you must use your own experience as your guide. We've all had these moments in our lives and the first step to recreating them is to be aware of how they made us feel.

SO HOW DO I GET ME SOME OF THAT?

I hate to open myself up to social criticism, but I am going to admit to you something that might sound like a character flaw. Please, no snap judgements. Here it goes: I like cats. There, I said it. And the best way I can think of to explain authenticity is through the a story of my own furry feline. Dog lovers please forgive the analogy. I promise it will be worth it.

My family had a cat when I was growing up, Kyoty. He wasn't allowed in our bedrooms at night but every now and then he'd find a door that was just open enough. He'd bolt inside and run straight under the bed. I would have to drop what I was doing to get Kyoty out of the room before my dad noticed he had broken the rules. It was basically impossible to do so, and made me extremely frustrated.

Around my 15th birthday, I finally understood that if I wanted get my cat out of my bedroom, I had to settle down, be super quiet, patient, and wait for my cat to ease himself closer to me. Some days it would happen in a minute or two, but other days he just won't come out, despite best efforts.

Authenticity is like trying to get a cat out from under a bed. The louder you yell, the harder you try, the more you grasp at a tail or paw to pull him out, the more likely you will fail. The cat will go deeper under the bed, press himself against the furthest wall or any space that is just beyond reach.

I set a goal to find a life that felt more authentic and then presumed that I would just grab authenticity by the leg and that would be that. Boom! Authentic self, attained. Now, as you know, it didn't happen that way—there was no instant success. I cried, yelled, pushed harder, worked longer, thought more, and did whatever I could to force my made-up timeline. And, like a cat under the bed, my authentic self slipped further and further out of reach.

It was not until I learned that authenticity required space, time, and patience in order to come out and be heard. And some days, even with all of that in place, my authentic voice did not lead me to an answer. Some days it let me know that I was still unsure—that I needed to consider my options further and should take a few days or get more information. Some days the answer was an obvious, "No!" Or a resounding, "Yes!" When that happened, I would try to follow up with a body scan to see how I was physically responding to the message the voice was telling me. I would also compare the way I was feeling to other truly authentic moments, like a sunset or the feeling of my infant son nuzzling against my chest.

In moments like that (and again, only you can say what those moments are) your thoughts slow down and you become truly present. You're not thinking ahead about what you have to do later, nor are you ruminating on something that already happened. Past and future don't exist. It's just you in that moment.

When you do find these feelings, it is important to connect with them in the moment. Notice how they feel on both a physical and emotional level. Then practice tapping into them on your own. Learning to reconnect to that feeling will teach you to connect to your authentic self. And it starts with slowing down.

And when I felt the urge to "grab the cat" I take these steps to slow myself down:

Start by becoming aware of your thoughts. Is your brain going a mile a minute?

Slow them down by focusing on your breath. Breathe in slowly, hold your breath for a second, and then exhale in a long, slow breath. Keep breathing in this way.

Allow your thoughts to pass through your mind, one at a time, without attaching to them or following them down the direction they may try to pull you. Treat your thoughts as though you are watching a movie.

Practice this every day for a few minutes so you can learn how to slow thoughts down at will. Then you'll be ready for the next steps.

Start Shedding Emotional Weight

Our negative thoughts—our impostor voices—are the things that have stood between us and realizing our true selves. This has happened because we have identified with our fear-based thoughts, mistaking them for who we actually are. Our true self brings us closer to the divine that exists in all of us. From there anything is possible and the groundswell of love, gratitude and faith is endless and forever available to us. The trick is how to cultivate the ability to listen to our emotional world and leave the rest behind. Most of us have some sense of this, but feel as though we have little control over it.

The goal of getting in shape emotionally is to become aware of what we think because what we think guides our lives. **Our thoughts determine our decisions and our decisions determine our actions. Our actions determine our lives.** This is why it is so essential to be aware of our thoughts and where they are coming from, to set intentions, make conscious choices and direct our actions accordingly.

Everything we need to make this change is already in place. We are already perfect because we were created in our perfect form. We are not lacking. We just do not have the patterns in place to access the parts of us that are able and ready for anything we want to achieve.

Getting in emotional shape is really about learning how to listen to our spirit, gut, soul, or authentic self, to identify and quiet the negative thoughts of our mind or ego. They never go away, but we can learn how to lessen their destructive effects on our lives. We want to allow the guiding light of our lives to come from our spirit, not our old, engrained, negative thought patterns. When we can begin to distinguish what our patterns are and that we do not have to let them lead our life's journey, our emotional fitness has taken hold.

Just like our physical fitness, our emotional fitness requires exercise—routines to help us manage our internal state—and healthy nutrition—the thoughts we "feed" our minds. That's what the rest of this book is about. It's a long-term effort to build and maintain the positive habits that will help us shed the weight and keep it off. And, just like starting a new physical fitness regimen, it can be hard to know where to get started.

My advice? **Start with what you want.**

Stepping on the emotional scale, acknowledging our emotional weight, and recognizing that our impostor voices exist can be overwhelming. So, let's start as simply as possible with a routine that will lay the foundation for shedding emotional weight and keeping it off:

1. Create space—Make your emotions a priority.
2. Identify what you want—Start with yourself.

3. Write a positive sentence—Begin with "I want," not "I should."
4. Call out your impostors—Notice how quickly negative thoughts arise.
5. Analyze the impostors—Are they in line with your beliefs?
6. Write a rebuttal—Make the impostors prove their validity.
7. Assess what you need emotionally—What do you need in order to move away from a disempowering perspective?
8. Identify actions you can take—Actions create change. What can you do right now to take steps toward what you want?
9. Take action! Start right away
10. Celebrate wins—Celebration strengthens the new emotional muscle.

Let's look at each step more closely.

CREATE SPACE

Just like physical workouts, emotional fitness routines need a time and a place. Create space in your day or week by setting aside a specific time to dedicate to your emotional health and stick to it regularly! Write it down in your calendar and treat it like you would any other commitment. Create a physical space for your workout too. Just as stepping into the gym or the yoga studio can put us into exercise mode, having a dedicated space for your emotional fitness routines tells your brain and your body that it's time to shift gears. Choose a place that is calming to you, as quiet and as free from distractions as possible. Make sure that you have a pen and paper (or a journal) handy too.

Treat the first few minutes after you sit down as your

warm-up. Breathe deeply. Meditate. Set an intention. Light a candle. Scream into a pillow. Anything that will help you to feel calm and ready to proceed.

IDENTIFY WHAT YOU WANT

Ask yourself, "What do I want?" It can be long-term, short-term, anything. There are no consequences. Pretend as if you have all the money and access and freedom in the world, what do you want? Quickly, write down anything and everything that comes to mind. Do you *feel* a desire anywhere in your body before you think it in your mind? Write it down. Do you feel resistant about any of your desires? Write them down anyway.

Remember, you're just putting pen to paper at this stage. There is no good or bad, no right or wrong; there is no room for judgment here. We'll get to those judgments soon but for now you're just making a list.

WRITE A POSITIVE SENTENCE

Look at the items in your list and pick the one that resonates most with you in this moment. If it is hard to choose, number them 1–10 based on the level of excitement you feel. In my case, my strongest desire was to write a book. **Now, write a positive sentence expressing your desire.** It can be as simple as, "I want to write a book."

Note: All too often, the idea of journaling or writing these things down can sound hokey to some of us; maybe it's terrifying to others. Do it anyway. When you write down your desires, you are bringing them into the real world. If you just answer the questions in your head, your responses and feelings remain in the abstract realm of your mind.

They are completely subjective there—you (and your impostor voices) can bury them, tap dance on them, and reshape them according to your fears—and it is very difficult to work with an abstract idea. By writing it down in a simple, affirmative sentence, you bring your desire into the objective realm. It feels closer. It is tangible. More importantly, it is actionable.

CALL OUT YOUR IMPOSTORS

At this point, your impostor voices have probably already started clamoring for attention. Give it to them. **Pull your impostors out into the open—into the real world—by writing them down as they speak to you.** Write down every sentence that starts with:

- "I would, but..."
- "I don't have..."
- "I've never..."
- "That's silly because..."
- "It will never work because..."

Write down every obstacle that stands between you and your written desire. Write down any reason you tell yourself not to get started. Do not judge them or their validity yet. Don't linger on any one item either. Write it down and move on as if you were taking roll call.

ANALYZE YOUR IMPOSTORS

As objectively as you can, look over your list of your internal obstacles. **Acknowledge them for what they are—impostors—and start to look for anything that they have in common.** Again, do not judge them as good or bad, true or false. This is a straightforward analysis. Do any of the items on your list make you feel a similar way? What is that feeling? Can you determine where that feeling came from?

When it came to my desire to write a book, my impostor list contained the following (among many others):

- "I've never written a book before."
- "My writing might be terrible."
- "I don't have a PhD."

What do these thoughts have in common? Well, I was clearly concerned with my lack of experience. It bothered me that I didn't have high academic credentials. I was afraid that my writing not be good enough—There is it. *Good enough.* I didn't feel good enough. Everyone has a "not good enough" sense. Mine was that I was not capable enough.

What traits do your impostors share?

WRITE A REBUTTAL

By now, your one positive sentence ("I want to write a book") must look pretty outnumbered by the impostor voices on the page. This is what emotional obesity looks like on paper—your true voice surrounded by impostors. And they're all talking at the same time. The positive message hasn't changed; it's just harder to focus on it because of all the noise around it. Let's give your positive sentence some support. **For every impostor voice that you have written down, write down a statement that refutes it.**

My rebuttals looked like this:

- "I don't have a PhD" = "A lot of writers don't have PhD's. I read and enjoy their books anyway"
- "I've never written a book before" = "Every author has a first book"
- "My writing might be terrible" = "This is my joy. This is my passion. My voice matters more than my grammar"

Practice these sentences. Repeat them to yourself. Revisit this page as often as you need to. These positive rebuttals will push back against the impostors in your mind—the judgments, anxieties, and learned values—and give your true self space to speak.

ASSESS WHAT YOU NEED EMOTIONALLY

What shared traits did you find among your impostor voices? What are the feelings behind them?

Did you find that you were feeling...

- Unworthy?
- Incapable?
- Unsafe?
- Unlovable?
- Insignificant?

All of these feelings are forms of lacking, of being Not Enough. Not worthy enough. Not capable enough. Not safe enough. Not deserving enough. Not loveable enough. Not seen enough.

When we are disconnected from our higher self and attach to the external world's view of what is Enough, we lose our ability to live in our truth. **We are enough because we are here—we cannot be wrong because that would mean we**

are made wrong. What made us is so far beyond our under-standing of the world and to say that we are made wrong is to say we understand what makes us. Regardless of your belief in God or science, you must understand that the very fact that you are *here* is amazing. We are enough because our hearts beat without attention and our eyes opened today.

This is something we have to attentively remind ourselves of. Left to their own devices, our minds move towards feelings of Not Enough as easily as our hands may drift to a bowl of candy. Without attention (and intention) Not Enough can become our default state.

Pay attention to how you are feeling in order to deter-mine what feelings are at the root of your imposter voices. Then figure out what you need to turn them around. Do you need to show yourself compassion? Do you need to give your-self love? **Once you have identified what you need, set an intention to give it to yourself and follow up with intentional action.**

IDENTIFY ACTION YOU CAN TAKE
What do you need right now? How can you give it to yourself? How can you practice it in your own world? Write down 3 things you can do this week.

In my case, I needed to show myself more compassion. So I asked myself:

What are 3 actions I can take to show myself compassion this week?

What are 3 actions I can take to show compassion to others this week?

The idea is to start small. Pick some things that are easily achievable.

TAKE ACTION!

Follow through with the actions you listed and write them down at the end of your day. How did it feel? Did any action in particular make you feel exceptionally good?

The 3 actions I listed to show myself compassion were:

1. Give myself permission to take a break when I feel tired.
2. Don't beat myself up for mistakes.
3. Set aside an extra 5 minutes for meditation after yoga practice.

The 3 actions I listed to show others compassion were:

1. Be kind and offer a heartfelt compliment.
2. Smile and ask someone about their day.
3. Find a way to be encouraging, especially if I feel inclined to be critical.

Each action I took gave me a boost but it was giving myself permission that made me feel the best. I set another intention to perform that action *again* every day for the rest of the week. **If any action you take makes you feel especially good, don't ignore it! Figure out how to integrate it into your life more often.**

CELEBRATE WINS

Every step that brings you closer to your true path is a win. And it deserves to be treated as such. All too often, we treat the end goal as the finish line—and only then can we celebrate and feel like we accomplished something. Let's change that. Every moment that goes well is an opportunity to celebrate.

That is not to say that I crack open champagne every time I show myself compassion or write a new paragraph, but I privately take a moment to smile, appreciate the opportunity and enjoy the possibility of what is to come. Every time I sit down to write, I am honoring my true desire and that is worth celebrating.

This routine can take a lot of different forms, depending on your emotional needs or even what you feel like doing on a different day. The important thing is to make your emotional fitness a valuable part of your daily or weekly routine. Make a commitment to it. This is the key to shedding emotional weight and keeping it off.

Part Two

Emotional
Nutrition

I scouted out an empty table in the atrium of the University of Chicago business school. I sat down, put Adele on, and stared at the computer. The blinking cursor on the empty page in front of me was terrifying but I felt resolved. I had committed myself to putting words on that page, to taking a step forward toward my goal of writing a book. As I sat there, the volume in my head began to rise. And it wasn't the soulful crooning of a 21 year-old Brit.

An imaginary buffet of negative thoughts was sitting right there. Like a chocolate-laden dessert cart, my thoughts rolled out in front of me:

"You cannot write without a PhD."

"What am I doing? I have a million errands."

"Look at all these business school students here. I should really go back to school."

"I should just get a job."

"It is cold in here. I am not comfortable. What time is it?"

I sat with my impostor voices for a second. *"I see you,"* I told them. I focused on my intention and tried to quiet my mind. I took a deep breath.

"Okay, sit. Don't get up."

"I'm going to die in this chair," the impostors fought back.

"First sentence. Here we go."

"I am going to die. This blank page is going to kill me."

But I did not get up.

Just as I know that I am responsible for my physical nutrition—the foods that I put into my body—I know that I am responsible for my emotional nutrition as well. The thoughts that we put into our minds (or allow to remain in our minds) have a tremendous impact on our emotional health and it's up to each one of us to determine whether we reach for emotionally healthy thoughts or emotional junk food thoughts. Giving in to the negative, self-defeating thoughts that were ringing through my head was as tempting as reaching for a slice of pie. It promised me instant gratification—I could give up doing this uncomfortable thing—and felt as good as any bad habit. I was determined not to eat the pie even though I could practically taste it. Today was the day to kick the habit of this style of thinking.

This was my moment of truth. The thoughts that stood between my goals and me were ready to have a battle, but this time I was ready to win. I knew that writing was something my true self desired to do. I knew my impostor voices would show up so I was ready to refute what they had to say. Most importantly, I understood that just because I have a thought does not mean I have to act on it.

The pie was in front of me but I did not have to eat it. I had a choice.

Modern Neuropsychology Agrees with the Ancients

The concept of Emotional Nutrition came as I began to understand the principles of Neuro-Linguistic Programming, or NLP. The theory, based on the work of John Grinder and Richard Bandler, explains the connection between neurology, language, and behavior patterns with the goal of helping people make changes quickly. In other words: how to make changes to our behavior by taking advantage of how our minds work with language. It tells us that our minds are simple input and output machines; they cannot distinguish between objective reality and our perception of reality, so when we speak negatively we feel negative. In other words, if we feed ourselves garbage we will feel terrible. Conversely, if we speak positively we will feel better. **We are in control of the stories we tell ourselves. We choose our reality.**

It was a message I needed to hear. At the time, I was still jobless, still spinning my wheels as I tried to put words on a page. I was lost and I knew it. In the midst of my seemingly endless quest to get somewhere I could only see the obstacles directly in front of me, the things that I needed to fix before I could take steps toward my goal. *I have to fix my inability to spell before I can be a writer. I need to read more; I should put together a reading schedule. I'm a slow reader; maybe I should take a speed-reading course* THEN *make a schedule.* I had actually convinced myself that I needed to fix my reading ability in order to write.

As this new idea sank in, I realized everything in the concept of NLP meshed almost perfectly with my beliefs, many of which were based on my favorite philosophical and spiritual texts. I was so excited. Could this recent idea in psychology really be this aligned with philosophy and spirituality?

In college, I studied Kantian philosophy. Kant was grappling with the same questions, but did not have modern science to help navigate how the brain works. He essentially states that we use our senses to perceive the world around us. We interpret the world through our senses and this interpretation dictates our worldview.

"What the objects may be in themselves would never become known to us even through the most enlightened knowledge of that which is alone given us, namely, their appearance."

— A43 CRITIQUE

If you take what Kant said and what NLP proves, the

conclusion is that there is no single truth in the way we experience the world. We are simply using our senses to understand the world—there is no right or wrong. In every moment our senses send information to our brains for interpretation: a comment a co-worker made, the way we look in the mirror that morning, the way our spouse spoke to us, even the way we experience our morning coffee and bagel. **The sum of all of these perceptions is the story of our life. You can choose to revisit any story and change your perception of it.**

Through our senses we create our perception and tell ourselves a story about how things "are." If that story can be told in thousands of different ways, then that allows for many different ways to view our lives. If there are many different ways to view our lives, then life becomes a question of how effective of storyteller we are. **How effective are you at telling a story that supports your life goals?**

NLP also explains that we naturally avoid pain and move towards pleasure. When we leave our unconscious mind alone to make daily choices, our decisions are organized around making ourselves feel good. This sounded familiar to another piece of philosophy I had read and loved.

As a student of philosophy, I read the yoga sutras. And, while there are a lot of them, I kept coming back to two in particular:

2.7. Attachment is that which follows identification with pleasurable experiences.

2.8. Aversion is that which follows identification with painful experiences.

I consistently returned to these sutras because they resonated with me; however, I had never figured out how to translate them into something actionable. That's the frustrating part about philosophy, philosophers never tell you how to implement their ideas. NLP did:

"People work perfectly. Our specific thoughts, actions, and feelings consistently produce specific results. We may be happy or unhappy with these results, but if we repeat the same thoughts, actions, and feelings, we'll get the same results. The process works perfectly. If we want to change our results, then we need to change the thoughts, actions, and feelings that go into producing them. Once we understand specifically how we create and maintain our inner thoughts and feelings, it is a simple matter for us to change them to more useful ones or if we find better ones, to teach them to others. The NLP Presuppositions are the foundation for doing just that."

— NLP: THE NEW TECHNOLOGY OF ACHIEVEMENT

On a late summer night, sitting on a porch in the final moments of daylight, I read this statement and laughed quietly to myself. We are working perfectly. We may not like the outcome, but we are not broken. Those outcomes are driven by actions, and actions are driven by feelings, and feelings are driven by thoughts. Life is not happening to us; we are completely in control. We need to change the thoughts that we allow into our minds—to feed our minds better—to produce a different outcome. **Change the thoughts and the whole system will change.**

I was in control. Better still, I had the power to change my unhappy situation. We are pleasure-seeking beings and, when left unattended, we'll avoid experiences that we *perceive* to be unpleasant. Our perceptions and perspectives can be shifted. I could consciously influence the choices I made by determining what was pleasurable and what was painful.

It was my breakthrough—my total Oprah A-ha moment. The message was very simple: We are not broken. Our lives are not broken. Our brains are machines, organized on a basis of simple input and output—we put in junk, we will get junk. By taking in thoughts that make us feel bad, we steer ourselves in the wrong direction; simply taking in thoughts that make us feel good will move us toward the results we desire. It was like choosing a perfectly ripe peach over a deep-fried Twinkie.

I began to think about the stories I tell myself as the emotional equivalent to the food I eat. I already understood that the foods I put in my body would impact how I felt and I knew the difference between what is nutritious and what would make me go up a clothing size. I found it was easy to think of my emotional nutrition in the same ways.

Positive, empowering stories will bring me closer to my goals. Judgment and negative feedback loops—emotional junk food—will add to my emotional weight.

Emotional Junk Food

We are aware that eating unhealthy foods, smoking, doing drugs or any other toxic thing we put into our bodies is bad for us; a nasty habit. Similarly, we have emotional habits that are causing discomfort in our lives. These negative thoughts and feelings are the chocolate cake and potato chips of our emotional lives. It takes discipline to resist their temptation until we break the habit.

To break a habit—any habit—we need to understand the consequences of continuing with it. The industries built around our physical health have very effectively educated us about the consequences our habits, both good and bad, can have on our bodies and that enables us to make a decision. If we smoke, we are told about the consequences and are made aware that the choice is ours. It may not convince us to quit, but we are aware of the risks.

Managing our feelings doesn't always seem like a choice—"That's just how I feel" is a common sentiment. Stuffing your mind with negative thoughts adds to your emotional weight just as stuffing your body with cake adds inches to your waistline. Negative thoughts can be especially impactful when we allow them to guide our actions or, worse, when we aren't even aware that they're driving our behavior.

Let's return to the smoking analogy (you can, of course, substitute your negative tendency of choice). And, for kicks, let's say you're going home to spend the holidays with your family. You go home with the best of expectations—to eat some turkey and see loved family members—but even the hardiest of people has experienced that moment of total infantile regression that happens en route to family functions. When you walk in the house, your mother gives you a look of disapproval over your outfit before you have even taken your coat completely off. You light a cigarette.

Within less than a millisecond, you find yourself filled with a wave of anxiety, then self-hatred about your outfit and aggression towards your mother. Without awareness of the pattern you're returning to, you sit in misery through the entire dinner. Another cigarette is lit. Maybe you begin to withdraw, go to the bathroom and cry, or find an opportunity to rip a good one back at mother. And, you smoke another.

The evening ends and you go home to rehearse the outrage you feel over your mom's comments. You vent to your spouse, you are up half the night replaying the evening's events in your head. The next morning you are short with the kids. Worse, you have taken the comment to heart and you are off to the store to buy new clothes because you feel awful about your wardrobe. You reach for a cigarette and—yep, the pack is empty. You smell like an ashtray and your chest hurts.

Maybe you do not call mom for a while for payback? You withdraw affections to punish her. This could continue for weeks, even months. You smoked a pack of cigarettes, but do you recognize that behavior as a pattern? You are in pain but are you aware of the cause? The negative emotional loop from childhood you thought you had dealt with is right there, reignited in an instant without any consciousness. Do you have enough awareness to know what this pattern is, or do you chalk it up to "Typical MOM"?

In this scenario, you caused physical harm to yourself and exposed yourself to negative emotional patterns that only add to your emotional weight. **This behavior is not you; it is habit. You can choose to stop being angry, just as you can choose to stop smoking.**

It is worth noting that we can become so accustomed to our negative emotional habits that we don't feel them hurting us. If a non-smoker were to smoke an entire pack in a single day, they would feel sick. But if that person smoked a pack the next day, and the day after that, and every day for a year, they would feel "fine". Their body would have adapted to the negative effect of their smoking habit.

If we are constantly reverting to our negative emotional tendencies, mindlessly reaching for emotional junk food like the pack-a-day smoker, our minds will adapt to them. With enough time, we can no longer distinguish them as something that isn't a part of our selves—they become impostor voices. We no longer realize how much they hurt us because we have become accustomed to their effect; we feel "fine". We don't realize how terrible we feel because we are smoking a pack a day without break.

We won't realize it until we stop.

I used to smoke (*Don't judge me, it was the Nineties!*) and I quit eighteen years ago and haven't touched a cigarette since... with only a couple exceptions. There was one instance that stands out in particular. Fifteen years had passed and I had been nicotine-free but after a couple of drinks and a long day at work I found myself accepting an offered cigarette. I lit it, took my first inhale in years, and—immediately started gagging and coughing. I couldn't believe I used to do this! Similarly, now when I give into my impostor voices and have an unfit day I notice the effects right away. I know what life feels like without emotional stress and the alternative—which had once been the norm—feels awful.

The desire to follow the impulse towards negative thinking is really powerful—it is as addicting as sugar, salt, or nicotine—but this is the beginning of real change. Sit, breathe, do nothing except observe the impulse toward this pattern and see that you have a choice. You do not have to follow in the same path. The pull to do the same action is powerful and any action will only feed it and make it stronger. Accept that this will not serve you in the end, create a desire for change.

The same is true for changing eating habits. In the beginning, it is very difficult to avoid foods that we should not eat, but over time, it gets easier and easier. Setting some guidelines for which foods we need to avoid is the beginning; understanding which emotions lead us astray will set the foundation for our emotional nutrition.

Judgment

"If you are pained by external things, it is not they that disturb you, but your own judgment of them. And it is in your power to wipe out that judgment now."

— MARCUS AURELIUS, MEDITATIONS

As I sat in the atrium of the University of Chicago business school, my buffet of negative emotions sitting squarely in front of me, I felt overcome with frustration.

What is wrong with me?

Why is sitting here making me so crazy?

I have always been undisciplined—I never did my homework.

Who am I kidding? I have nothing interesting to say.

I don't read enough.

I am not a good writer.

What is my writing voice?

What if I say something stupid?

Maybe I should meditate to find my voice.

My overall feeling was, "What is wrong with me? I should not have these thoughts." I was judging myself. Harshly. Judging my thoughts only made me judge myself more and the cycle continued, leaving me paralyzed—stuck. Rather than judge my thoughts, I needed to listen to them and decide if they were saying what I truly believed.

The words of Marcus Aurelius rang between my ears: "If you are pained by external things..." (Yes, I definitely am) "...it is not they that disturb you, but your own judgment of them." I sat back in my seat. The Stoic philosophers dating back to 3rd century BC were right. Judging my ability to write based on external ideas about what defines a good writer left me a victim to ideas outside of myself; therefore I could not do anything about my circumstances. If I took what the Stoics suggest seriously, I could feel better immediately by getting rid of the internal judgments. Of course, that is easier said than done.

It was bad enough that I had to call out my impostor voice telling me that I should open another business when, in fact, I wanted to write. You would think it'd be enough to fight off the impostors; that I was done when my moment of clarity came. Nope. As soon as I located my true desires I started to judge them, too. Now, I had to battle my own judgment.

Our judgment voices are rigid, "right and wrong," "good or bad" stories. Assessing anything in those terms can quickly bog down anything you want to do. The secret is that your true desires cannot be wrong. Others may disagree or desire a different life. **Remember, it is your birthright to design your life.** You may make a mistake or may even fail, but it is your right to try to create the life you desire. Therefore, judging yourself for your thoughts, goals, and desires is a useless activity. Focus instead on the outcome you want and the kind of story that will empower you to achieve it.

In this way, ancient wisdom from the Toltecs dating back to 900 CE comes to our rescue:

"The inner Judge uses what is in our Book of Law to judge everything we do and don't do, everything we think and don't think, and everything we feel and don't feel. Everything lives under the tyranny of this Judge. Every time we do something that goes against the Book of Law, the Judge says we are guilty, we need to be punished, we should be ashamed. This happens many times a day, day after day, for all the years of our lives."

— MIGUEL RUIZ, THE FOUR AGREEMENTS

If we are adhering to other people's ideas of what we should feel and think, then we are holding ourselves to a "Book of Law" written by someone else—and punishing ourselves for straying from someone else's path. I realized I was punishing myself because the true desire of my heart conflicted with what my imposter voices were trying to dictate. Thinkers from Ancient Greece to Early Mexican civilizations have all said the same thing: stop judging. And they were right.

In my work with clients and in my own process, I have found that the largest barrier to our emotional nutrition (after accepting that unconscious negative thoughts are destructive) is the harshness of our internal judge. My clients locate their true thoughts and desires, but then immediately judge themselves so intensely for having them that they don't move past that point.

One client works tirelessly instead of spending much-desired time with her children. One afternoon she admitted that she does not want to work so much, that she neither needs nor wants more professional achievement. She recognized that it was her impostor voices that were telling her to achieve more at the expense of her personal time. It was a huge realization! However, it only took about a millisecond before she started judging herself for wanting to work less; a minute later, she was calling the idea "idleness". She wants to be home with her children and work less and she has the means to do it, but her inner judge does not allow it.

I understand her frustration very well. All too often, when I experimented with an idea, I would receive the same message. I would judge the worthiness of my idea (it always came up short) and would judge myself as not good enough.

These judgments are learned values.

The challenge is to begin to distinguish between the thoughts that are impostor thoughts and those that are true to our authentic self. Our judgment comes from a collective voice based on the views of those who have taught us. As the impostors infiltrate our minds, we create rules about what is right and wrong. Even when we go against the rules that we have been trained to believe as true, we judge ourselves against them.

My advice? Notice the words you use: "Should." "Right." "Wrong." "Silly." "Stupid." "Impossible." "Can't." When you locate what you want to do, notice how quickly you destroy your dreams with judgment. Determine whether it is your own judgment you're concerned with, or the likely the judgment of others. **Assuming that others will judge you is as debilitating as judging yourself**.

So how do we battle judgment?

Give your ideas a moment to exist without judging them. Whatever you want needs to survive without judgment, especially in the beginning. Assume you are not going to do much today except dream about the new path. Judgment is not as strong when we are not faced with a need to take immediate action. Say what you want a few times and notice how the judgment rushes forward.

Judgment is chocolate cake. It's there. It's tempting. But you don't have to eat it. When judgment starts to creep in on your thoughts and desires, don't dive right in but don't ignore it either. Notice the cake but don't eat it without thinking about it first. What will it feel like if you give in to its temptation? Do you want the outcome of eating the cake? What is the thought and do you believe in what you are hearing? Slow down the process and tune in.

First, notice a thought, any thought. Take a deep breath. Attempt to find a quiet moment, even if it is just in the car before going into work. Close your eyes and breath deeply into your belly and relax any parts that are holding tension. Notice anything. Refrain from judgment. Simply become aware of your thoughts and allow them to come and go like changing channels on a television. You may notice one thing on your mind or many. It does not matter. What matters is that you notice them and practice detaching from them. **The moment you can watch a thought, even if you only watch it for one second without judgment, you have located your authentic self. This is the part of you that you may call your heart or your gut. The part of you that notices the thought is your authentic self.**

It's a simple concept but the execution is very challenging. Much like breaking any habit, we have to dig deep and not fall prey to endless cravings. Our job is to nourish our authentic self by avoiding judgment. **Our inner judge wants us to believe that our gut, our authentic voice, is wrong or misguided rather than allow that part of us to believe in the abundance of the world and our abilities to achieve whatever we desire.** Yes, we must work. Yes, we must sacrifice. Yes, we have to find ways to achieve, but first we have to be able to dream.

Determine what you want or what you want to change.

This is your life. Don't judge your desires. Give yourself the time and attention to determine what you truly want. What is your goal? Create a mission statement. *I want to be a great mother. I want to be an amazing cook. I want to be a communicator.* It can be anything.

Why do you want it? *Because I want my children to have an amazing childhood and go on to be global citizens of the world. I want to communicate my ideas to help people.*

Allow those thoughts to exist. You don't have to take action yet—just let them be and stop any judging thoughts that try to sneak in.

Remember, judgment is a waste of time and causes the wheels of the machine of your life to grind to a stop. If we can look at our thoughts without judging, it gives us the opportunity to make a choice. When we make a choice, we take our destiny into our hands.

Negative Feedback Loops

As I sat in the b-school and attempted to write, I kept feeding myself my favorite junk food thoughts. **Each of us has unique sentences to convince our selves that we are not enough**. We all share in some version of this negative self-talk and unconsciously allow it to lead us down the same old path filled with regret and frustration. I told myself: *I do not have the expertise to write. I am not ready. No one will like what I have to say. I should get a "real" job.* I had crafted unique sentences to feed myself. These sentences led to feelings of being overwhelmed, a desire to quit, and a lack of self-confidence. I was trapped in a negative feedback loop.

Negative feedback loops are the result of emotional junk food eating habits and they are as easy to slip into as a plate of greasy chicken wings. The stories I told myself all fit nicely into one sentence: *I am not good enough.* And, as I told the same stories over and over, I reinforced the negative feelings. It takes discipline to resist the opportunity to feed our minds junk foods thoughts.

I have a lot of self-confidence but, because I was feeding myself so much junk food emotionally, I eroded my belief in myself. To overcome this feeling I would reach out to loved ones, thinking that if the consensus was that my ideas were good enough then I would feel better about my own self worth. I had outsourced my sense of self to something or someone. My identity, my self worth, had become dependent on the responses of others. **In other words, I no longer determined the outcome of my life because it now belonged to the beliefs of other people.**

When it came to writing, I had a lot of supporters. Thankfully. Finally the views of the external world fit with my own desires. As I called one friend after another and sheepishly explained my ideas for my book, I got positive feedback. They were offering me nutritional thoughts that allowed me to move forward. By accepting the views of friends and family I was able to break out of my negative feedback loop.

I would get off the phone and return to my computer screen. Using the momentum of a friend's alternative voice, I would type a few more sentences. However, my craving towards my junk food thoughts was so strong that I would inevitably return to my original thoughts creating an unbelievably deep feeling of low self-esteem again. With this incredibly painful negative loop would come equal levels of self-judgment: *What is wrong with me? Clearly, I have no talent, given how little I am doing. I should forget all about this.* Just as the voice of judgment would nearly consume me, I would call another friend for some inspiration and so it would go.

We all know the feeling that comes after we eat more than

we should. After we indulge, we must judge. This self-abuse is so much worse than the caloric intake. We feel ashamed that we let ourselves down again by breaking the diet; frustrated that we probably gained weight. We eat junk and then we self-abuse. Our bodies are filled with a toxic diet and our minds are filled with toxic thoughts.

What do we tell ourselves that keeps us in this place?

I do not deserve.

I am not lovable.

I do not have enough.

I am not safe.

The world is always a disappointment.

Nothing ever works out for me.

I am not capable enough.

Everyone has his or her own type of negative looping.

"Why am I in this relationship? S/he does not treat me well. What is wrong with me that I am staying here? I deserve better. I hate myself for staying. I am afraid to leave. I am afraid to speak up and defend myself."

"Why am I staying in this job I hate? I will never get another job that pays well. I hate going to work every day, but I cannot deal with change right now. I can deal with my job as long as I get to have a glass of wine at night."

"Why am I not taking better care of myself? I never have time for me. I always take care of everyone else, but I do not remember the last time I did anything for myself. I cannot keep giving out at this pace, but I have no choice. I have to take care of others. No one understands how stretched I am. I cannot do less or everything will fall apart. I am going to get cancer if I do not find some time to take care of myself. I just can't now."

It is a story that we tell ourselves. The first step toward breaking that pattern is to learn to listen to our unconscious negative looping voice. From there, we can train ourselves to hear the negative messages we tell ourselves and the long stories we use to justify our positions. Hidden behind the stories we tell is a disempowering global belief that covers the common human experience that we all feel: *I am not enough.*

A version of this global belief is the umbrella statement that becomes our life lens. My lens came in the form of "not capable enough." I had so many stories about writing and my capacity to write—about what makes a good or a bad writer and what a real job looks like. The truth is that I was simply repeating the same message over and over. I am not capable enough. My story was my way of avoiding the shame that came from feeling that I was not enough. Once I read Brené Brown's work on shame in *Daring Greatly*, I realized that this is a huge part of the human experience and I was not alone. I did not have to waste time with shame because everyone feels the same way.

I started walking around in the world looking at people as if they had little balloons over their head. Each one would be a different "not enough" statement. Not thin enough, not rich enough, not powerful enough, not capable enough, not smart enough, not lovable enough, not worthy enough. You can almost see it in people's eyes when they speak. It seems that just about everyone has a fear that they are "not enough" in some way and yet we believe that we are alone in our experience!

Take a moment to look at the stories that you are telling yourself and the feedback loops you are caught up in. Are those stories really code for one of the statements above?

Isolate the patterned thinking, the sentence you tell yourself and decide if it is what you want or if it is just a disempowered global belief. If you cannot isolate the umbrella statement, the centerpiece belief behind your story, write down all the sentences you say when you experience fear, anxiety, resentments, guilt, shame, unworthiness, lacking capability, grievances, anger, or depression. See if they would fit in one category. If not, that is okay. Work on telling a new story.

"I CAN'T LEAVE"

Relationship problems? Either you cannot find someone to love or you are not connecting to the person you are with. What is the story you tell? What is the sense behind the story? Is there a fear? Is there something you feel you are lacking? Begin there. Write a new story that outlines all the ways in which you deserve love. Having trouble. Try seeing a coach. If you don't want to call a coach ask a friend to help you draft a new story.

"I'M NOT READY"

A common story is that you would move forward on a project, relationship, change of job, but you are not ready. There is a long list of reasons why: kids, money, and obligations, to name a few. Maybe the reasons you cannot make the change are real, but mainly I find that the reasons are carefully crafted stories to justify a deeper fear. I swore I could not make the move away from my old job for a lot of reasons. In reality, I could, but I was covering my fear of change. I wanted to be certain that the end result would be perfect before I moved forward. It's a lovely thought, but it's also an impossible one.

We cannot know the outcome before we begin. Life is too uncertain. We can set an intention towards a desired outcome and take steps toward that goal.

"I DON'T HAVE TIME"

Another common story is that you would or should change jobs, relationships, or take better care of yourself, but you do not have the time, money or opportunity. Again, sometimes we have more obstacles than other times, but this story is mainly a way to avoid admitting the fear of the unknown.

To avoid the discomfort of change, we use emotions like blame, anger, or resentments. The distraction of these emotions avoids the vulnerability—we are afraid that we will not be okay in some way. **The solution is a deeper trust that your inner guidance will steer you in the direction you desire. Simply put: you begin to trust yourself.** This simple idea requires us to access our inner voice, something I had lost connection to long ago. I could not trust in something that I could not locate. By removing the junk food thoughts and replacing them with nutritional thoughts, I started to reconnect to my inner voice—the only space that accurately guides me through my life. It never fails me and it is always available. I just had to learn how to locate it amongst all the noise in my mind.

I want to make sure I am not giving the impression that I cut out all emotional junk as soon as I understood the concept of emotional nutrition. As I mentioned, shedding emotional weight and building healthy habits takes effort. I was grocery shopping with life coaching classes in my iPhone, in the bath with spiritual leaders playing on my Mac, and even asked God for the answer in my meditations. I would work a little and then the voice of judgment and failure would chase me out of my still point. I would quit for weeks and then try again in complete frustration. Finally, like quitting smoking, I just swore off the negative thoughts. I decided that no matter what they told me, I was going to write. And, let me tell you, me and my negative patterns had a really big fight. Old habits and cycles can be hard to break.

Let's look at how we can move out of the cycle of emotional junk food and change our stories to positive, nutritious beliefs that will empower us toward the desires of our true selves.

Storytelling

"Emotion from the pain-body quickly gains control of your thinking, and once your mind has been taken over by the pain-body, your thinking becomes negative. The voice in your head will be telling sad, anxious, or angry stories about yourself or your life, about other people, about past, future, or imaginary events. The voice will be blaming, accusing, complaining, imagining. And you are totally identified with whatever the voice says, believe all its distorted thoughts. At that point, the addiction to unhappiness has set in."

— ECKHART TOLLE

The stories we tell ourselves on a regular (even on an hourly) basis can have a powerful impact on our lives—for better or for worse. Whether we're aware of it or not, we are always thinking, interpreting, and contextualizing everything around us. These thoughts—the voices in your head—create a story. In the above quote, Ekhart Tolle explains that telling ourselves a sad story will make us feel sad. An angry story will make us feel angry.

The quality of our stories impacts our happiness. We carry them with us, allowing them to be the filter through which we view our world and, as Tolle suggests, we probably don't realize how strongly they are impacting us. We identify with the voice, even if we are not consciously creating the story. And if we don't change our stories, they can consume us.

When I was introduced to Neuro-linguistic programming, NLP, my world of potential broke wide open. After all my years of struggling to make a change, it finally felt like a *possibility* rather than a faraway hope. **I learned that we are all storytellers. We uniquely perceive the world in each moment and create stories based on these perceptions. Every moment of life is an opportunity to interpret the world and in each of these moments choose to see things in new ways.**

Here's an example: My son calls for me, interrupting my quiet morning (those precious few minutes) just as I've sat down with a cup of coffee. That is one story, but it isn't the only story available to me. I can look at it another way: my son loves me and wants my love at the start of his day—trading my hot coffee and quiet for warm coffee and a hug doesn't sound so bad. My trip to the grocery store can be a nightmare of traffic and frustrations or an opportunity to cook for my family. **Many things happen in a moment and all of them are potentially true.** Since they are all potentially true, and are all are happening, why choose to focus on nightmare traffic if I can choose another perspective?

We improve our emotional health when we can let go of the stories that are disempowering and create some space for a story that is empowering. For example, I had a story that I had been telling myself since high school: I did not work that hard as a teenager and ever since I have been playing catch up. The idea that I am always trying to catch up creates the feeling that I am not good enough.

I made a small adjustment to the story and changed my entire perspective. My new story was that I had a slow start in school, but hit the ground running in college and never looked back. The second story focuses on how I have moved on; the first story left me with the sense that I never did. Change the details of the story a little and we change the emotional response. It's a choice. From this choice, I can build a life based on my heart's desire.

What about the stories that we tell ourselves that we believe we have gotten over? What about the stories that were painful? The stories that we do not like to think about but we know are there. The moments that a parent was not there for you or someone hurt you or let you down. A defining moment in which a coach or a teacher told you that you were not good enough, or a friend told you that you have no style. Maybe it was a parent that did not give you the attention you needed. A moment that defined who you believed you are.

These stories layer and layer around our true self until we can no longer hear its voice. They can overtake us if we are not careful. We are not our stories, but we can become our stories. Hour after hour we analyze, assess, ponder, worry and become anxious or depressed about circumstances out of our control. We cannot control the weather, illness, other people's behavior or other events in the external world, but we have a lot of control in our response.

The greatest minds from the East to the West tell us

to become clear about what you control and what you do not control. We do not control events outside of us, but we do control our response to those events. Our sense is that our response is limited by the external event, but our responses are infinite. In most moments, you can decide to interpret the moment in a wide variety of ways. We already know this. We know because other people interpret the world differently than we do. So just as you would not immediately dismiss the alternate viewpoint of another person, try to understand your experience from a wide variety of perspectives.

When we take the time to set clear goals and intentions, we can observe our true voice and our negative patterned thoughts. At that point we can decide which one we want to listen to—old negative thoughts or current intentional thoughts—when we make our life plans and decisions. This is the process of being responsible for what we think because we accept that our thoughts determine our lives. We have a choice to live unconsciously allowing our old patterned thinking, impostors, to be our guiding voice. We can also choose better for ourselves. When we accept responsibility for our thoughts, we open our world to anything we desire.

I have found the most important thing is to refrain from rehashing a negative moment (or my offended perspective on it) through the day. I am the author of my thoughts and when I am not, I will pay the price. I've learned that the more I retell the story, the unhappier I get. Conversely the quicker I let my negative story go and move on with my day, the happier I am. If that does not work, I have to tell a better story!

Avoid being overtaken by your story by listening to the way you frame a moment. Events happen and we see them as a difficulty. That difficulty can help you grow and learn, or it will cause you to become resentful, angry and stuck. A marriage that has been challenging for years can be the greatest opportunity to grow. A loss can be an opportunity to try something new. A death can be an opportunity to awaken to the fragile nature of our own lives.

I reframed my story over time. There were so many parts that I had identified with that did not belong to me. They were layered on top of my dreams, so I had to start to peel them off. It went like this:

EMOTIONAL LAYER #1: WHO QUITS A GOOD JOB?

I have the opportunity and I am going to take advantage of it. Many people would give up a lot more to follow their dreams. I am grateful that I can.

EMOTIONAL LAYER #2: WHO WRITES A BOOK WITHOUT FANCY DEGREES?

I have always been interested in this subject. I have read far more than most people on this topic. I have lived the books I have read.

EMOTIONAL LAYER #3: YOU HAVE NOTHING OF VALUE TO OFFER.

Yes, I do. I am happier now and I have found a way to feel better. My coaching clients are reporting huge changes in their lives.

EMOTIONAL LAYER #4: I AM GOING TO TRY THIS OUT AND IF IT DOES NOT PAN OUT, I WILL GET A "REAL" JOB.

Nope. This is my job. I am a writer. I am a philosopher. I have to do this. It is in my soul and it is where I can add the most value in the world.

We can enable ourselves to tell that good story by becoming conscious of the stories we have created. If they are empowering, keep them; if they are disempowering, write a new story.

WHAT IS YOUR NEW STORY?

Just pick something that is not working exactly the way you had hoped and write it down. Then write down why it is not working. Read through what you've written and determine: What is the story?

Once you have isolated your story notice the language you use, the way that you explain what is not working. Have you told yourself this story for a long time? Does the story involve blaming others? Does it involve a sense of helplessness? Does it include anger? Most areas of life that we are stuck in include these types of feelings. Are there alternative ways to interpret this area of your life?

Emotionally Healthy Thoughts and Actions

"Yesterday I was clever, so I wanted to change the world. Today I am wise, so I am changing myself."

— RUMI

If you want to make your life better, you have to start with yourself. All too often we look to the world outside of ourselves when we're looking to make a change in our lives. If only our environment was different, or our schedules were more conducive, or our partner was more supportive, then we would find the outcome we want. Rumi is raising the age-old idea that trying the fix what is out there will never work. The world does not bend to us. We have no control over the world around us, but we have total control over our selves. By changing ourselves, we can change the world.

Health is not just about removing the junk food out of

our lives; it is equally about adding foods that nourish us. The nutrients in food fuel our bodies to provide the energy we need. Similarly, nutritional thoughts provide the energy needed to accomplish our daily tasks to live a full life.

Junk food causes harm to our bodies. Junk thoughts cause harm to our emotional lives. Removing them stops their destructive impact, but it requires us to replace them with something healthy. When we add nutrition to fuel our emotional lives, we are energized and excited to step into our lives fully.

Every morning we wake up and brush our teeth because during the nighttime hours bacteria build up and increase the chance of tooth decay. Our bodies are aging and each day we have to work against the natural progression towards decay. The same is true of our emotional world. Without attention, our emotional states degenerate. We have to wake up and check in with our emotional lives to avoid emotional decay, just as we need to brush our teeth.

What is the emotional equivalent of a toothbrush, vitamins, or egg white sandwich on gluten-free bread? Culture does not effectively define the means available to us to manage our emotional health, but there are many out there.

If we are supposed to eat green leafy vegetables, which one of the dozens out there do you like? How do you like to get protein? In other words, we know the choices we can make to eat healthy and have figured out how to do so in a way that is palatable to us. From the options available we pick a combination that supports our health. It's not about being perfect; it's about being well. We have the skillset already and it translates perfectly to our emotional health. **Let's set our goals for emotional wellness, not emotional perfection.** Let's aim for optimal, holistic health. It may not add years to your life but it certainly can increase the quality of the years you have.

So pick some emotionally healthy thoughts and actions to support your emotional life on a daily basis. Do you like to journal, meditate, jog, kick-box, or do yoga? Do you like to set goals and work with a coach to manage obstacles? Do you read self-help books daily and set the ideas into practice? Do you like retreats, workshops, or inspirational blogs? Do you practice a religion or spiritual ideas? There are so many ways to add emotional nutrition in your life.

My emotional nutrition comes from ideas, a great quote or a new perspective from a friend. I also love setting goals. One week I decided to see how many times I could catch myself making assumptions—I lost count around 100. I put myself on a "cleanse" to try to break myself of this emotionally unhealthy habit. By the week's end, I had made tremendous progress. Just like I attempt to avoid certain foods and eat something more nutritious, I approach my emotional world the same way. I've found that focusing on an emotional cleanse, of assumption, anger, or grudge-holding, for a week is extremely effective at kick-starting my emotional weight loss. Then, practice, practice, and more practice are required to break the habit.

What can you take from any of these areas and incorporate into your life daily? What action can you take? Until I understood that I needed to take action, instead of just studying the concepts, I saw little improvement. We brush our teeth daily and eat healthy food—these are daily actions—and we need to create daily habits that promote emotional health and make us feel great. Without taking regular action, we will not see the benefits.

Connection

I sat with a devil on my shoulder for some time, listening to the endless lists of reasons to quit, but I did not move. I looked across the atrium and I saw the father of one of my son's classmates sitting just like me, writing. But there was one small difference between us: he was very content. I just sat there, staring at him and wondering how anyone could be that happy writing.

Finally, my curiosity got to me and I walked across the large atrium to find enlightenment. He greeted me pleasantly even though I had interrupted his blissful meditative space. I just weirdly blurted out, "I want whatever you have."

He laughed and asked me what I was talking about. I said, "How do you just sit here and write without either running, crying or throwing your computer across this beautiful atrium?" He asked if I ever read *The Artist's Way*. I had not. He smiled and said, "Quantity, not quality and God will take care of the rest."

Clearly, I had taken what little space he had to offer because he was in the midst of something amazing. So, out of respect to his future contributions, I smiled and walked back to my seat, thinking, "That's it??" At the time his answer didn't feel like a revelation. It was, however, an entirely different perspective than the one I was approaching my writing with. And it felt *good* to talk to someone about what I was struggling with, even for just a minute. Brief as it was, it was a connection—and I felt energized by it.

Connection is a way to feed our minds positively while actively taking a step toward our goals. Sometimes it is as simple as asking others who have already achieved the goals you hope to attain how they did it.

Do you know a parent you feel is parenting the way you want to? Ask them what they are doing. Ask what they believe in and find out how they are parenting the way they are. Can you talk to the businessman who has made the money you desire? Is there someone you know who followed her dreams? Ask her how she achieved what she did and what she told herself to pursue those dreams. If they are happy with the outcome, I am confident it did not come from negative thinking. The sentences they are operating from will be about gratitude, joy, and service. Talk to others who have achieved what you would like to achieve. Find out what they do.

Are you a people pleaser? Do you have trouble saying no? Ask someone who says no all the time how she does it. What are the exact words and phrases she uses? What is her perspective on saying no? The details help. I had a client who could not refuse a friend's requests for coffees when she had work to do. She felt bad and did not want to upset the friend by rejecting her. We came up with a sentence she did feel comfortable using: "Let me check my calendar and I will get back to you with some times." This gave her the opportunity to schedule herself first and avoid all the negative thinking that came along with denying her needs in the face of others. Sometimes an outside perspective can make all the difference.

Are you impatient and need results immediately? Do you have conflict in your life because others are always falling short of your hard driving nature? Find someone who is really patient and ask him or her how they maintain composure. Learn from those who are strong in the areas you wish to improve in. Listen to their advice and try it out in your own life. Sometimes the thoughts we'd never consider are the ones that get us where we want to be. That was certainly the case for me.

Quantity, quantity, I thought... I heard the voice in my head telling me that I am not a writer and I should get up. I was not going to chase the old pattern that gets me nowhere. *Quantity, Quantity*...I started to write. I wasn't trying to make anything sound good; I just wanted to put words on the page. I wrote and wrote for as long as I could. I was responsible for my thoughts and I was choosing to think differently. I was choosing not to take action from my thoughts. I was not going to eat the pie. I would look up all the time, desperate to give in to the urge to quit, but I told myself to just keep typing.

Somehow an hour and a half went by and I had written two or three pages. Most importantly, I had interrupted the pattern. I called my partner of 14 years at work and told her that I had done it. *I wrote.* I began to read what I had written. As I read I heard the words. I heard the voice. Tears rolled down my face as I continued to read.

The hardest part of beginning to write for me was this idea of what voice to use. I had assumed I would find a voice that sounded like someone who writes books. Now, as I read, I knew I had overcome this obstacle but not in the way that

I had anticipated. I recognized this voice. It was *my* voice. I could barely read as the tears streamed down my face because I was so overjoyed. My voice, the one that was never good enough, the one that could not write, was right here on the pages. And I liked her.

I am responsible for my thoughts. I did not have to follow the negative, disempowering stream of judgment and self-criticism. I could do the opposite and, even though, I had no faith that I would succeed, I did something different. As I released myself from the thoughts that had unconsciously consumed me and replaced them with thoughts that would empower me, my true voice—the one that had always been there—spoke clearly, loudly and just like me. The only way I can be.

Eating unhealthy foods feeds our bodies in an unhealthy way. Thinking negative thoughts feeds our spirits in an unhealthy way. When you stop eating unhealthy foods you help the body get healthy and when you manage your thoughts you help the spirit get healthy. When we shed the weight of thoughts that were unfortunately and often unintentionally brought into our lives, we move towards our true self.

We do not want to change who we are, we simply want to get closer to our true selves by bringing awareness to our learned behaviors, so we can stop acting from this place. We were born free from judgments of right and wrong. We want to free ourselves from the weight that keeps us from our true voice, our true selves. When we can act from that place, our home, we will always be home. **Know that anything that comes from a negative thought will only lead you to a negative place. Practice speaking to yourself from a place of self-love, faith, gratitude, and joy.** The result will be finding our true voice, spirit and faith in the divine.

Part Three

Emotional
Fitness

In our emotional lives, isolating the change we want to make is half the battle. Then, the emotional workout requires finding the tools and exercises that work for you.

We experience emotional weight in different areas of our lives: relationships, finances, work, health, or personal wellbeing. I began my journey believing I had an issue in my work life. I wanted an authentic job, but, in truth, I struggled with managing my sense of my capacity. This question of my capacity could have emerged in my relationship or in my financial planning. For me, it happened to come up in my belief in my career abilities.

No matter what is weighing you down, the goal is to incorporate emotional fitness into your daily life with workouts designed to shed the emotional weight and make you feel lighter, happier, and more joyful in your life. When it comes to our physical fitness, we have to have a workout plan: cardio, strength-building, and flexibility. Typically, we assess what we want to improve to determine our fitness goals. If we want to lose weight, we may increase cardio; if we want to get stronger, we lift weights.

What do you want from your emotional fitness plan? What do you want to improve? Do you feel weighed down by feelings of unworthiness? Are you carrying the weight of unresolved anger? Are you overwhelmed? Do you feel there is never enough time to take care of yourself or all the things in your life? Or are you not sure? This section addresses common junk food thoughts with an emotional fitness workout. Read through the different junk thoughts to see if they sound familiar. If so, it may be the workout for you. Maybe there are several that apply. If that is the case, you can work through each of them individually or combine exercises.

Physical fitness and emotional fitness are similar. We have to get rid of bad habits that are not in line with our goals and values. With physical fitness it may be bad eating habits or never exercising; with emotional fitness it is being unaware of our imposter voices and the impact those voices have on our actions that interferes with success. The goal is to replace the bad habits with better ones. Choosing healthier foods and exercising more will get you in better shape, and nutritional thoughts that support your desires will improve your emotional health. That's what these exercises are all about.

My breakthrough came when I finally understood that general positive thinking did not help me. It wasn't enough to break my old patterns. I had to understand the junk food thoughts that were influencing my actions and determine their cause. What were the actual sentences I would use to create the emotional state that led me down the same old path over and over? When I understood what my sentences were, I had to replace them with nutritional thoughts that were specific to my thought pattern. Specificity and personalization are the keys to internalization.

Our issues with our jobs, relationships, lack of personal time, finances, or any other external issue, rarely have to do with the issues themselves. They are all the symptoms of a deeper problem within us. I was not simply having an issue with finding a job. There were plenty of jobs out there. I was repeating the same thoughts to myself over and over. These thoughts were about me and they were about something I felt I lacked. When I replaced these self-doubting thoughts with new ones, everything fell into place. I had to start with me.

Check out the sentences below and see which ones resonate. We are looking for the junk food thoughts that are most common for you, or the ones that you want to start with. **Many of us eat more than one junk food and many of us have more than one type of junk food thought.**

Find an area that you want to start with and read about the subject. The more you understand your junk food thoughts and the benefits of changing your habits, the more motivating it will be to do so. Then, it becomes a process of removing those junk food thoughts and replacing them with more supportive nutritional thoughts. At first, your mind and body might resist—it might be really difficult—but it gets easier quickly. Plan on resistance. It is a workout after all. Workouts can be challenging, but that does not mean it is bad or wrong to do.

Getting into emotional shape will require mindfulness at first. Just like exercise, it will become a valued habit over time as you start to see the benefits of your increased fitness.

Emotional Workout #1: Anger

Anger is like a mosquito bite. It feels so good to scratch, but when you do it itches more and eventually bleeds, scabs over and can leave a scar. If you struggle with anger, this is the section for you.

Do you hear yourself saying:

- That person deserved what I said.
- He/she can get away with that @&$#, but not with me.
- Who does he think he is?
- No one talks to me that way.
- I taught him respect.
- I put him in his place.
- He will think twice about talking to me that way next time.
- S/he needs to hear how they made me feel.

Pema Chödrön, a Buddhist monk, turned my life around with her work on anger in *Don't Bite the Hook*. Pema suggests that anger baits us and we have to make a conscious choice not to bite the hook. When anger arises, we need to learn how to manage the pull it has over us. We have to accept anger the moment it arises. Learn to notice anger and how it feels in your body. Then, learn how to experience anger without taking action. Allow anger in and then allow it to go.

Often the anger is so explosive that the time between the external trigger and your reaction is less than a second. Before consciousness has a chance, your anger has taken off and words are spewing in the direction of another. And, your child, spouse, neighbor, friend, or colleague is either fighting back or crushed from your inability to manage the moment.

Maybe you feel guilt or regret afterward, but maybe not. Maybe your justification for your anger is so strong that a story kicks in, convincing you that you did the right thing.

Getting angry is easy. Not getting angry—not indulging in the reaction—is much harder. It is especially hard when the truth is that we feel scared or hurt. When I react angrily, it is usually because I am only masking hurt or insecurity. To avoid speaking my truth and experiencing more hurt, I use anger to protect myself.

Anger is not right or wrong. **It is an indicator that someone has triggered something within us that needs investigation**. We would not be angry if the incident or comment did not touch something that was vulnerable. There are dozens of comments that are not bothersome, so why would one comment suddenly arouse such a large response? Our belief is that the other person or event was truly wrong—and maybe they were—but when an angry reaction gets ignited in you, ask yourself: "Did I react this way because there is something within me that was wounded?"

Miguel Ruiz addresses this beautifully when he says:

"You may even tell me, 'Miguel, what you are saying is hurting me.' But it is not what I am saying that is hurting you; it is that you have wounds that I touch by what I have said."

As Ruiz says, the question we should ask ourselves is, "Why did that comment hurt me?" instead of, "What can I do to set this person straight?" Most of the time, we are hurt because of the meaning we apply to someone's actions. It spurs on a storyline of what is right or wrong leading us to feel upset or angry.

It feels easier to lash out at someone if we believe that they are actually trying to hurt us. In reality, however, that is a story we tell ourselves to justify (and perpetuate) our anger. The more likely scenario is that the other person is not actually trying to hurt you as much as they have a story about how you have behaved that has ignited something in them. They want to say or do things to you because of their own inner dialog. Even in that event, outbursts of anger will not resolve the issue. You may want to avoid that person or consider how you will deal with them, but aggression only leads to more aggression. Setting firm boundaries to deny any further access this person has may be needed, but using anger as a weapon will not result in anything more than more destruction.

Another misunderstanding is that anger shows strength. It doesn't. An outburst is not strong; it is a loss of control. The stronger choice is to set boundaries and not allow others access to your life when they behave badly—getting angry is the easy way out. To kick anger you have to be courageous.

Real courage is to speak from the heart in moments of vulnerability. Give it a try, if you think you are strong enough.

Those of us who are prone to outbursts of anger need to learn how to contain our emotions until we have the ability to say something that will not lead to a destructive outcome.

What has anger done to your life? How many people have been negatively impacted? How has it affected your health? How many scars do you have? Which relationships have been destroyed or what has the impact on your children been? What about the way it has affected your work life? If you think about it, the outburst of anger has not done anything productive. Even the person that you believe you have confronted and "taught" a lesson has probably not changed.

WHAT ARE THE BENEFITS OF MANAGING MY ANGER?
Have you ever thought about the amount of hours you have wasted being angry? Once I realized that anger was just depleting me emotionally and causing my work and life to suffer, I started to rethink the value of anger. I could wake up in a great mood but then get angry with someone or something and ruin my day. I'd head down a path of negative emotions that distracted me from other goals, sleep, or my relationships. The outcome of my anger was my own unhappy day.

"Holding onto anger is like drinking poison and expecting the other person to die."

— BUDDHA

Anger causes you to repeat the details of the incident over and over, prolonging your unhappy mood. I was the queen of holding onto those moments until I realized that I was devoting my energy to it, *making myself sick*, yet the person I was angry with had no idea. I was drinking poison and expecting the person to die.

Anger is a great opportunity to identify your emotional weight. By getting curious about what is going on inside *you*— the pain points that were kicked up—you can learn the source of your anger and take steps to neutralize it.

ONE-LINE STRATEGY
An angry outburst will only hurt you. Get curious instead.

EXERCISE

1. Slow down
2. Become curious
3. What else are you feeling? Guilt? Hurt? Sadness? Fear?
4. Stop judging what you cannot control.
5. Understand your boundaries. We can only control our self.
6. Add lots of compassion

For a few days, the only goal is to say nothing. As you experience anger, turn inward and notice how your body feels. **Slow down. Become curious.** What is happening? Are your shoulders tight? Is your chest heavy or tight from quick breathes? Is your stomach in knots? How about your eyes? Are they intense, like they are popping out of your skull?

Once you have found the physical effects from the anger, try to relax that part of your body. Take deep breaths and focus on releasing tension. Movement helps. Can you get up and go for a walk? Can you do a forward fold? Do anything you can to relax your body.

Next, listen to your story. What are you thinking? What is the emotional junk food you're feeding yourself right now? Are you offended? Are you the hero, the one to stand up to the aggressive people of the world? Were your feelings hurt? Was your pride hurt? What is the story you are repeating that justifies the response you're having?

Go a little deeper. Cut the other person out of the equation and focus just on yourself. What else are you feeling? Do you feel sad, hurt, unloved, not seen, not worthy? Can you identify why you feel that way?

I read The Four Agreements: "be impeccable with your word, don't take anything personally, don't make assumptions and always do your best." I understood the missing ingredient. Anger was happening because something got sparked within me. I got curious. *Why am I upset? Yes, I was offended. Yes, the person was rude. Yes, the action was just wrong, but why* **this**. *Why am I losing it with* **this** *specific situation?*

I took an inventory of the feelings that could be behind my anger: guilt, feeling manipulated, feeling hurt, or feeling afraid. What was it? What was the invisible junk food that I was consuming?

Everyone is different. We do not have the same responses because we do not tell the same stories. The story you are telling is causing your pain—it is the itchy mosquito bite that you are scratching. Stop making it worse. Change the story.

Consider the object of your anger. Remember that you have no control over the other person even if you "give them a piece of your mind." When you do that, your goal is to change them, to change their perspective. It's not possible to inflict change on someone else by telling him or her what you think of them, you can only talk about you. **You can explain how the event made you feel, if you choose to do so**.

The same approach applies in recurring clashes. Are you stuck in an endless loop with someone? A fight that began years ago and continues? One that dies down but then resurfaces time and time again? These sorts of loops typically occur with a loved one—the ones we tend not to just cut out of our lives. The same rule applies in these scenarios as they do with someone you are not close to: You have no control over the other person. Judging their behavior without trying to figure out why it made *you* upset will simply leave *you* stuck. Your anger and judgment do not create change. They only create resentment, more anger, shame (being judged sucks), feeling unloved, more hurt.

If you focus on controlling your mind, not the person you are angry with, you will find true internal strength. This is the ultimate core workout. It's painful, but the strength you create will carry you a long way.

An alternative is to get clear with your self first. What upset you? Then, the power over our mind comes in the form of a new story. Tell a story that gives you the space to continue forward. We don't want to be stuck. We don't want to lose days, weeks, months even years of our lives feeling bad because of the actions of other people. We do this because we tell stories that trap us rather than free us.

When you are really mad, what sentences do you use to get really wound up? What moments cause you the most pain? What are your anger junk food thoughts? Take a moment and write them down.

My Junk thoughts were:

- I can't believe she said that. Who does she think s/he is?
- I may be nice, but I do not get taken advantage of.
- He has met his match.
- Nobody does this to *me*.

Once I realized how little impact my anger had on others or situations and how it actually took time and efforts away from my life, I went on a detox—no more poison for me. However, there was one small problem with my detox program: I had no plan for how to handle those moments when someone else's anger was in my face. My detox went great until someone cut me off in traffic or a family member said that one thing that stirred years of bad habits of anger within me.

First, I thought about the junk thoughts. Do I believe in them in principle? They really were junk. When I listened to myself, I really heard how petty and obnoxious I sounded. If I heard anyone else talk like that I would not agree with it. By asking myself if I really believe what those thoughts are saying, I realized I did not.

Emotional fitness requires having a strong emotional core. An emotional core is a core set of beliefs that I take action from. The core of me knows right from wrong. It knows when I am acting out of fear rather than compassion or love. I just don't always listen. The emotional workout is to act from the emotional core.

NUTRITIONAL THOUGHTS
Do any of these thoughts sound like a good fit for you?

- Anger is toxic—I am not toxic.
- Anger is destructive—I am not here to destroy.

- Anger is only a mask to avoid real feelings—I am strong enough to show my real feelings.
- Anger is a copout—I do not take the easy route.

I started my emotional workout by choosing nutritional thoughts from my core beliefs. These sentences are much more closely matched to my emotional core. How do you view yourself? Are you an honorable person? Do you have high levels of integrity? Are you kind? Are you loving? How does anger fit with those morals? Is anger in conflict with your higher self?

Anger gives me a headache—I care about my health and wellness.

Anger has never worked in the past—I do not waste time with things that do not yield any outcome.

Anger feeds my ego, but not my soul—I work from building self, not feeding my ego.

How can you reframe your junk thoughts to create a nutritional and empowering new perspective for yourself?

My reframed my perspective on anger to say, *"Anger is toxic and destructive—I am here to build, not to destroy."*

Once you have determined the nutritional thoughts that you connect with most, add a vision. According to NLP, when the nutritional thought is combined with a clear mental image, your odds of success increase dramatically. An image combined with a personal statement allows for an alternative that you care about, creating space to move past the old behavior into the new one.

"First, make what you want to do and what you think about into a positive statement. Second, increase the mental vividness of what

you want to do in order to increase its attractiveness for you. And third, associate into these successful behaviors and mentally rehearse them, so they feel natural. This step-by-step program approach is a hallmark of NLP."

— NLP: NEW TECHNOLOGY: THE NEW TECHNOLOGY

Finally, remember that compassion is the best prescription for anger.

Once you have replaced you negative thoughts with nutritional thoughts, it's time to show compassion. When anger strikes and we slip down the rabbit hole of justifications for our anger with our well-crafted set of negative stories, we lose our connection to the recipient of our anger. You know those moments when you are so angry that you replay the scenario in your head a hundred times. In those moments, you are lost in your own mind. There is no longer space for the person or situation that caused the anger. You have no compassion for the human being you are interacting with.

Try adding some compassion back into your inner dialog. Can you see the humanity of the person you are so angry with? Can you see the inner struggle that caused them to behave in a way you did not like? Maybe it was not a person that upset you, but some external unjust moment. Regardless of the cause, try to find some compassion. The truth is that everyone is suffering and tapping into their suffering and finding compassion diminishes the anger.

Compassion for others is also compassion for our self. Each time we find compassion within for others, we strengthen our emotional health. We take a step closer in connecting to our higher self and believe in our own ability to act from that space.

Look into the eyes of your "aggressor". Can you see the pain in their eyes? Can you see that their words are coming from their own fear or hurt feelings? Can you move past their words and see the person behind them?

One morning, I was driving to Michigan for a quiet weekend with my family on a Saturday morning. A man was in the middle of the street blocking traffic in both directions. I honked my horn to see if he would move over or move forward. He did not. After some time, I was able to pass him. As I was driving past, I stopped and looked into his car window. He rolled his window down and began to swear in my direction. And when I say he began to swear in my direction, I mean he strung together a list of profanities that I would have never believed could exist in the same sentence. I like a good swear word, but this really was impressive. Typically, this would stimulate an equally aggressive response from me to prove that I am not a push over.

That morning, I stopped. I watched him swearing, but it felt like someone turned down the volume. While he went off, I saw his worn skin and a look of defeat in his eyes. I imagined his life matched what his expression exhibited: a life of many obstacles and pain. As I was lost in my moment of compassion for him, I would come in and out of consciousness only to be reminded his volatile rant was not over. Without having anyone to respond to his anger, he slowly became conscious of his vicious verbal attack. His face began to drop and he seemed to take on a look of embarrassment.

Compassion worked. I left without comment. More

importantly, I left the man and his words on the road. I drove to Michigan free from his pain.

TAKE ACTION

Awareness is critical to making a change. What types or events trigger your angry junk thoughts? **Next time you are in that moment, come prepared with your nutritional thoughts.** Repeat them to yourself and pay attention to your body. Where does the tension begin? You are creating a new habit. Your body and mind are ready to fight you—relax them. Practice resilience to the emotional discomfort.

Are you angry about an annoying situation, like being stuck in traffic? Think about how you can use the time for yourself. Catch up with a friend; listen to an audio book; do deep breathing; sort through a challenge; or just enjoy some silence.

Are you angry at the incompetence of another? Practice compassion. Remember that you don't know the other person's experience. Maybe they had a crisis that day. I choose to believe people are doing the best they can with what they have—some days we just have less resources than others.

Are you angry with a family member? Determine how *you* are feeling. Are you hurt? Disappointed? Scared the relationship is in trouble? Is your anger masking another feeling? What else is happening? Do you need to separate yourself from this person for some time? It is better to remove yourself from the interaction than to build up resentments. You have a choice. And if you would fare better from a permanent separation, you can always end the relationship, even with a family member.

Are you angry about an email correspondence? Don't fire

an email back. Wait. Breathe. What bothered you exactly? Does this other person warrant a response? Explain how the other person made you feel, if you want, but adding anger to anger is angry.

And, of course, in all these situations ask yourself: what is the junk food thought?

Even after you have calmed down from the heat of the moment, dig deeper into the core of your negative reaction. This is your junk food. It is like looking down at a big plate of french fries or chocolate cake. Do not take a bite. Notice it, but come back to your nutritional thought. Envision yourself and how amazing you will feel without carrying this emotional weight. Repeat your nutritional thought over and over and practice showing compassion.

Emotional Workout #2: Harboring Resentments

Anger without expression is still anger and it still causes harm. If you are hiding anger or feel you are able to move past upsetting events quickly, this section is for you.

Do you hear yourself saying:

- I am not angry. Sure I sometimes feel frustrated or angry, but I do not act on it. I move on.
- Conflict is uncomfortable.
- I avoid awkward emotional moments.
- No one will really care or listen to my feelings so why voice them.
- I am fine. I have no need to express my feelings. I just move on.

Anger turned inward has to go somewhere. Much like a balloon filled with water, with enough pressure your anger has to release. Engaging in difficult conversations or creating conflict is seen as a negative quality so some resort to avoiding their anger at all costs. Again, anger itself is not a problem because it is an indicator that something does not feel right inside you. When used as an internal gauge, it can be a very useful tool. That sense, that feeling, could be telling us a truth that we are in fact in danger and should avoid a situation. However, avoiding the feeling by stuffing it down with the goal of being a good person only leads to one end: an unexplained outburst at another time.

The pressure of avoided feelings must be released somewhere. Maybe it is later in traffic, or an unexplained outburst towards a friend, child or spouse; maybe it appears as unexplained depression or intermittent crying privately. Whatever the case, the anger has to be released. All of these "unexplained" feelings could be unexpressed anger.

ONE-LINE STRATEGY
Stop stuffing—it will only result in an explosion.

EXERCISE

1. Feelings of anger are not bad
2. Conflict can be cleansing
3. Emotions are healthy to express and can be done with grace.
4. You are entitled to your feelings.
5. Other people's feelings about your emotions are their problem.

Next time something happens that causes some discomfort with someone or something, try to sit with the emotion for a moment. You may have the desire to get up and distract yourself from the emotion, but try to sit with it for 30 seconds. Does conflict causes you anxiety? No need to create conflict, but what about sitting with your emotions? Can you stay with it for a moment?

What are the junk food thoughts you are immediately thinking? Do you need to run? Do you want to yell, but you are too much of a people pleaser to consider that option so you avoid? What is the process?

What does the experience of sitting with your feelings feel like? Does it feel tight in your chest? Is your stomach heavy? Anxious? Do you want to cry? You are allowed to have your feelings now. Remember the more you allow yourself to feel now, the less accumulation you will have later.

The reality is that the same advice is true for anger whether it is turned inward or expressed outwardly. Something is triggering you and you need to resolve this issue.

How many times have you not expressed yourself? How many times have you come up with the short-term excuse that the conflict was not worth it? How many times have you felt okay with that choice and then found the weight of the emotional stuffing creeping up later?

What will it feel like if you continue to stuff down your feelings? How will it affect your relationships? Who has it hurt later when you are venting old frustrations? Avoidance is the attempt to withdraw from what we do not like, but avoiding the feelings within ourselves is the issue. The unresolved anger becomes toxic and heavy. The issues that you feel you have avoided are still there.

The goal is not to become an outwardly aggressive person, but to reflect on the emotions and make a decision about how you want to proceed. Often curiosity, as explained in the previous section, can be the cure for avoidance. Ask a question. Make sure you understand the person or issue facing you. Are you making assumptions?

Maybe someone has voiced a frustration that is making you uncomfortable. Ask a question. Get some clarification: "What did you mean when you said..." "Are you upset with me? Did I do something that is making you angry?" Maybe share your feelings. Explain your emotional distress. Could you share that you feel nervous or anxious about the situation without blaming?

How amazing will it feel when you say something, anything and walk away without that extra weight? How proud will you be that you found your voice? Throw away the word conflict. You are not avoiding conflict you are speaking your truth. Begin with a question. Gather your facts and, once you are sure that you understood the other person, express yourself. It is your right to speak your truth and when you free yourself from your self-imposed prison of resentment, you will feel freer than you ever knew possible.

NUTRITIONAL THOUGHTS
Do any of these thoughts sound like a good fit for you?

- I do not avoid.
- People I love have good intentions.
- I may feel fine in the short-term, but I don't want to take shortcuts.
- I love clearing the air.

- Sharing feelings is not conflict. It is just sharing thoughts.
- People who love me value my feelings.
- I am safe.

TAKE ACTION

Take one thing that bothered you and express yourself. Is there a particular incident that you still think about? Could you express yourself? Try saying, "I am sure you did not mean anything by this, but when you said _____, it hurt my feelings," or, "When you said _____ I took it to mean _____. Is that what you meant?"

Try one. A little clarification can go a long way.

This exercise is all about the reps to create new emotional muscle! Create a new habit of expressing the things you truly feel. It will be difficult at first, but the more you practice, the less resistance you will feel. Find as many small opportunities to approach someone or something you are avoiding. Remind yourself that you are safe. Remind yourself that your opinion matters and that you deserve to be heard. Keep doing this until it no longer requires a conscious decision. You are getting stronger every day!

Emotional Workout #3: Neglecting Yourself

Self-care is so vital to our health, yet it is often one of the first things we will neglect.

Do you find yourself saying:

- I don't have the time to work out, take a bath, or get a massage/manicure/pedicure.
- I should be doing something else.
- I can't do _____ because I will disappoint someone.
- If I do not get this work done or take care of this person, everything will fall apart.
- Taking a bath, walk, exercise, meditation, is indulgent.
- Working more and meeting other people's needs is a sign that I am successful.

When we make appointments with others, we work hard to honor the meeting time. Yet when it comes to the time we slot out for ourselves, assuming we even do that, we cancel on a dime. It feels indulgent to bother taking care of our physical and emotional lives when there are so many other important things to do.

Self-care is so essential and yet it's a very easy thing to set aside. "I don't have time," feels like a perfectly viable reason for neglecting our personal desires and needs; sometimes it even feels like the "right" thing to do. We claim, "I would exercise more, spend time with friends, family, take a walk, but I do not have the time." As we continue to deprive ourselves of these things—the needs and wants of our true selves—we condition ourselves to ignore them. It is as unhealthy as depriving our bodies of water or basic nutrition.

I WOULD TAKE CARE OF MYSELF, BUT I DO NOT HAVE TIME
When we stop taking the time for our self-care we create a deficit. Think of it in terms of dehydration: when we go for too long without water, we begin to feel a noticeable effect in our bodies. We feel thirsty, our skin feels dry and tight, and if we continue to deprive our bodies of water, the symptoms become much worse and much more painful as the deficit grows and more areas of our bodies are affected. Stay dehydrated for too long, and your body will begin to lose its ability to function effectively. We have to replenish that deficit before we feel better and the amount of water required to do so increases the longer we stay dehydrated. If your body has been regularly deprived of hydration, a single glass of water isn't going to cut it anymore.

Let's face it, over time we all know what happens when

the nights and days of self-neglect start to add up. Our moods, health, relationships, and work begin to suffer. These are symptoms of the deficit we have created by neglecting our needs and desires. It is easy to misconstrue the message they're telling us, however, because we have been taught to dedicate our time and energy to external things is the right thing to do. So rather than recognize these symptoms as a need for internal focus and prioritization, we convince ourselves that they are a sign that we need to do more work externally. We believe we need now need to dedicate *even more* energy to save the relationship, get the promotion, and stuff down our moods.

And the deficit grows.

Eventually, like a dehydrated body whose systems are slowly shutting down, we begin to do everything less effectively. Our sense is that we are working hard, but we are seeing a diminishing return. This is because we are neglecting the very thing that allows us to be effective. If we continue to look outside of ourselves for the solution, sacrificing our time, energy and focus to external things—more work, another commitment—we can begin to feel trapped by them.

What we choose to spend time on becomes the very things that we feel held captive by; however, we are not victims of our life choices. We can and we must make the choice to take care of ourselves.

TAKING TIME FOR YOU IS NOT SELF-INDULGENT. IT IS NECESSARY.

How often do you sign up for "just one more thing" because you feel like you should? How many of your activities are necessary? How many recharge you and make you feel good?

The one thing I hear from my clients the most is that they don't have the time to do the things they want to do for themselves. It goes like this:

I want to...

1. Become a great chef
2. Garden
3. Run a marathon
4. Have kids
5. Open a business
6. Change directions
7. Get in better shape
8. Be a better parent
9. Be a better spouse
10. Be a better friend
11. Take better care of myself
12. Travel
13. Take a workshop
14. Write a book
15. Take a nap

Most people's lives look like one long laundry list of things to-dos. At one point I had several lists: my home list, my work list, my wish list (everything that will never happen), and the list in my head that never made it onto paper.

All my lists were overwhelming and URGENT!

How great would it be to step into your days with a sense that you picked your life and most things are happening because you *choose* to do them, not because you feel like you *should*.

Have you asked yourself, "Where did this to-do list come

from anyway?" The list that says we have to do this or that? *A handwritten note after a dinner party is necessary. My child's haircut has to happen every 8 weeks. I have to volunteer more, even though I am never home for dinner.* **We made up those rules.**

Have you thought about what you commit your time to? Is it in line with your values and goals—your internal motivations? Or is it just something you heard a friend is doing, an external motivation that arbitrarily says you have to do it too?

What if you did something insane and started with you? What if you scheduled in yourself first? What would that look like?

I had to ask myself those same questions. I try so hard not to break a promise. If I am meeting someone, I try to honor it; if I take on a project, I try to deliver. What about my commitment to myself? Why wasn't I as committed to myself as to others? That had to change. I decided to start with me. I looked at my schedule and decided that I was not controlled by my life; I am the owner of it. I sat down in front of my computer and scheduled me first: my writing time, yoga, and time with my family before I scheduled other commitments.

The truth is that there are few things I have to do, the rest are choices. I have to take care of my child and make enough money to live on while planning for the future, but that is it. Everything else is a choice.

If I volunteer my time, it is a choice.

If I exercise 3 times a week, it is a choice.

If I cook dinner every night, it is a choice.

If I spend 4 hours a day watching TV, it is a choice.

If I socialize several hours a week, it is a choice.

If I work more hours, it is a choice.

It is our choice to work more, to achieve more, and to have

more. Bigger houses, several houses, vacations, cars, clothes, jewelry, and dinners out are all luxury items. We don't need them, but we may want them. The important thing is to determine whether you are making these choices because of internal motivations, or external ones.

When I stopped feeling like a victim of my own choices, I felt better about my life, even when I was very busy. I changed the way I thought about my commitments and I changed my feelings about them. I like to achieve, so I work. I like to feel healthy, so I workout. I love being a parent, so I spend time with my son. I love being in a relationship, so I spend time on it.

WHAT ARE YOUR CHOICES? WHAT ARE THE PRIORITIES IN YOUR LIFE?

Some days I am up early and really busy. However, at that moment when I want to feel sorry for myself, I remind myself that my busy day is my choice. If I want to have less, I can do less. A simple reminder that I am busy because I choose to be reenergizes me to push forward. Notice the next time you begin to feel overwhelmed by your schedule and see if a quiet reminder of your motivation helps.

Prioritize yourself first. Take a moment to look at your next week's schedule and carve out time for yourself. What do you love to do? What do you want or need? A trip to the gym? A round of golf? A walk or hike? A hot bath? Meditation? A manicure? A nap? Some time with a book or a movie? Schedule time that you will take care of yourself. Really! Get out the calendar as if it were a meeting with someone important (because you are important) and schedule that time.

If you wake up at 6:00 am every morning and go to bed at

10:00 pm to get the necessary 8 hours of sleep recommended, you have 16 hours of time awake each day. To say that there is not 30 minutes of time for yourself is to say that you have taken on too much. Cancel someone or something else.

ONE-LINE STRATEGY
Schedule you first. You matter as much as anyone.

EXERCISE

1. Schedule you.
2. Manage disappointment.
3. Others can and do wait.
4. You design your life. Change your rules.
5. Add some self-compassion.

Take out your calendar for the day, week or even better month. Schedule some time for you. Unless there is an actual emergency, this time cannot be moved. Schedule exercise, a coffee date with a friend that you want to see, a massage, or whatever replenishes you.

Give yourself permission to take this time. If you take the time and spend it worrying that you should be somewhere else, then there is no reason to do it. The whole idea is to enjoy your time. What rules are in the way from experiencing joy and freedom for a few minutes a week? What have you convinced yourself MUST be done? These are your junk food thoughts. They have to be removed and replaced with something more in line with your core beliefs.

NUTRITIONAL THOUGHTS

Do any of these thoughts sound like a good fit for you?

- Taking care of myself is just as important as everything else.
- If I don't take care of myself, everything else suffers.
- Self care is not selfish.
- I can disappoint others and the world won't end.
- I choose my life design.
- I can make changes whenever I wish.

Remember this is your story. We tell stories. I had the 80-hour workweek, the child at home and the relationship that was getting zero attention. I did yoga, but felt like I was indulgent. As soon as I finished and I had a moment of happiness, I would role up my mat and RUN to the next meeting. I felt bad that I was unreachable for an hour and my solution was to compensate by working harder for the next 2 hours. In other words, I replenished myself then immediately drained myself of all that newfound energy. What was the point?

I had to rewrite my story into one that empowered me to choose myself.

NUTRITIONAL THOUGHTS

Do any of these sound like a good fit for you?

- Every day I make choices—I am not a victim to my own life.
- Every day I can change my choices—I make choices that make me happy.
- My needs are as important as other people's needs—I can take care of myself.

- I have one hour this week for me.
- My kids, spouse, boss, friend, email, voicemail, laundry, dinner, can all wait one hour. This is my time.
- I can say no to other people's goals.

I am a grown up. If I don't take care of myself, who will? I want to live a long healthy life and I really hate feeling stressed, tired, and overwhelmed. Therefore, why am I giving myself over to some external set of rules about how much time and effort I should put into everything other than my personal wellbeing? If my goal is to work hard and feel good, why would I work tirelessly and feel terrible?

Work is important and I want to be a success. But if stress and misery come part and parcel with that "success" then I need to look elsewhere. True success will not leave you drained and unhappy. It will not force you to neglect yourself.

The best remedy for lack of self-care is self-compassion. We practice compassion for others but not for our self. It's not easy to do; showing sympathy, kindness, care, concern, warmth, and humanity toward ourselves is not something we have been conditioned to do. We express concern for others. We can see when they do not look good from stress. We are happy for them to get in a workout, even jealous. Why not express the same level of support for our own self?

TAKE ACTION
This week, schedule time for you. Can you come up with one thing this week that will be just for you? How else can you pare down your schedule? Are there things that you are doing that you do not need to do? Can you cancel something or

quit one committee, commitment, or appointment that is not necessary?

Create as much time for yourself as you can and make it a high-priority appointment. This time is unmovable. Pretend like it is an appointment with the President of the United States if you have to. Do not cancel on yourself.

As you take action into the week, notice what you say to yourself to deny yourself this time. Repeat your nutritional thoughts over and over—give yourself permission to take care of yourself.

REPEAT FOR SUCCESS

As you try to dedicate more time just for yourself, you may find that you are fighting yourself. You may find yourself rationalizing away your extra 30 minutes, or cancelling your gym class because sometime important came up. That is okay! No shame. No judgment. Keep trying. **You are creating a new habit and it will take time.** As long as you are caring for yourself even a little bit more each week, it is progress. You are losing those emotional pounds!

Emotional Workout #4: Blame

"If you are distressed by anything external, the pain is not due to the thing itself, but to your estimate of it; and this you have the power to revoke at any moment."

— MARCUS AURELIUS, MEDITATIONS

Do you hear yourself saying:

- I was in a good mood until...
- I would be happy if...
- My parents did _____, so my life has turned out _____.
- I would have been, happier, more successful, a better communicator, better at financial decision maker, but...
- If only s/he _____, then I would _____.

We cannot control the world around us. Life is hard and there is not a lot you can do about it.

"I am really the nicest person in the world; it is just all those other people and events that have caused my unhappiness. I would be happy if only..." If you have something or someone who you would fill in, then you need a blame detox and some healthy nutrition on what you can control and what you cannot control.

Blame. I love to blame others. The truth is that a lot of people and events are really annoying. I woke up in the best mood and then as little events happened my mood deteriorates: traffic sucks, my car stalled, my spouse said something really annoying, my child is sick, a friend called to complain for 20 minutes, my mother and father, well that list is so long that I don't have space. My fabulous mood that I was in is gone. I am bitter, depressed and or any other emotion that is anything, but happy. And it's everyone else's fault.

Before anything can improve, the victim mindset has to go. We all have the victim voice within us, but as often as possible it needs to be checked. **We are not victims until we adopt the victim mindset.** The victim within us wants us to say, "This is happening to me and I have no influence to change it." We always have the ability to change something in our lives, even when it feels like we do not. Yes, there are times when we are truly stuck in a terrible situation, but those who inspire us the most are those who find their way out without being a victim. They learn, grow, vow to have better in their lives, keep hope alive, still trust, still love. This is what we should aspire to do as well. But the victim mindset wants us to shut down. Give up. If that happens, we let go of our ability to step forward into the world and live a life we desire.

The important thing to remember is we have full control over our mindset and very little control of what happens outside of us. I never stopped to think about what I had control over and what I had no control over. There were so many things that I was worrying about that I had no control over like other people's behaviors, moods, feelings, likes and dislikes; and while I was so preoccupied with these things, I did not have the emotional energy to recognize what I did have control over, me. I can always control myself. I can choose a thousand things to do. I can be loving. I can say something kind to someone. I can walk away from someone. I can move. I can get a divorce. I can quit my job. Spending time blaming someone for my mood is like waiting for Santa to get me what I want for Christmas at 43 years old.

If I blame others for my mood, then I have no control over my mood in any given day. If someone or something can influence experience at any given moment, then I am hostage to the world around me. I am a victim to whatever comes my way. Let's face it, the world is not always pleasant. Once I realized I was outsourcing my daily experience to the world around me, I knew I had to make a change. I wanted to be happy when I felt happy and sad when I felt sad. I did not want to be controlled by external forces that I had NO control over.

How many years have you lost blaming external things for your current situation? How much time has gone by? How much of your life have you missed? What if you continue to blame? How much more time will you lose? How many people have you disappointed? How much have you disappointed yourself by sitting in blame mode without taking action to make a change? What could you do if you stopped blaming and took action? How would that impact your life?

ONE-LINE STRATEGY

You control you—no one can make you feel anything unless you let them.

EXERCISE

1. Remove the victim.
2. Take control of your thoughts.
3. Be proactive—not reactive—What do you want? Blaming distracts from planning next steps.
4. Set boundaries.
5. Blaming has not outcome.
6. Add some gratitude.

Is there a person who "makes" you feel a certain way? Attempt to spend 60 seconds with that person while you maintain your happy state. Think about puppies or kittens until the 60 seconds are over. Once you have made it 60 seconds, abruptly walk away. It is okay. Celebrate that you made it for 60 seconds without handing over your control. Once you can successfully manage your mood for 60 seconds, try 90 seconds.

Notice the story you begin to tell about the other person and how they make you feel. Practice awareness of this story and where you feel it in your body. Do you feel your heart race? Do you feel your palms sweat? Tightness in your chest? Tension in your shoulders? Do you feel down or anxious?

"Reactive people are also affected by their social environment, by the "social weather." When people treat them well, they feel well; when people don't, they become defensive or protective. Reactive people

build their emotional lives around the behavior of others, empower-ing the weaknesses of other people to control them."

— STEVEN COVEY, SEVEN HABITS OF
HIGHLY EFFECTIVE PEOPLE

You may not like someone else's behavior, but you have no control over them. When the problem exists within someone else, we have no choice but to remove the pain of the experience. The pain can only be diminished if the other person agrees and takes the action you desire.

Since you do have control over your own behavior, what choices do you have? When you change your focus from what the other person has to do to remove your pain and focus on the choices you have, you take control and create options. You can always walk away. You can tune the person out. You can show compassion for them. You can express your feelings about the person's actions from the first person. "I feel hurt by your words." "I am experiencing a lot of aggression or frustration or guilt or shame in this moment."

Does the weather determine your mood? Do you hate it when it rains? Invest in some really good rain gear. Try journaling—rain inspires good writing. Throw a dinner party. Rain and red wine with a fire go well together. Again, take control over what you can impact because changing the weather is not possible. In some areas, like where I live, the weather is a chronic problem.

My moods are always my choice. I am in control of one thing at all times, me.

EMOTIONAL WORKOUT #4: BLAME · 149

SET BOUNDARIES

One of the most effective things I picked up in my emotional workout was the exercise of boundaries. Other people are just passing by me like scenes in a play. People are not doing anything to me. They are living their lives. Sometimes the way they live can annoy me. Getting mad at them or sitting in judgment does nothing to my situation other than leave me stuck and complaining.

I began to determine where people were coming from—the dark side or the light side. You can tell in an instant. The dark side sounds like blame, shame, anxiety, insecurity, anger, passive aggression, and/or resentments.

Remind yourself: I cannot control someone else's mood; I can only control my reaction to it. Don't get sucked down into the dark side. Try to surround yourself with people who bring positive emotions into your life. By positive I include sadness with vulnerability or anger with vulnerability. We have bad days, but there is a difference between those who are victims to it and swim in the negativity verses those who need a friend. Be there for a friend, but don't get taken down.

"Where focus goes, energy flows. And if you don't take the time to focus on what matters, then you're living a life of someone else's design."

— TONY ROBBINS

Next time someone is "making" you feel a certain way, remind yourself that you are choosing to participate. You can always choose not to. Really, walk away. Tune them out.

I found that blame was an excuse for me to stay stuck. When I spent time—and I could really spend a lot of time blaming—all I did was complain. What did I really want? What need was not being met? What was the obstacle? Outside of blaming the person that appeared to be causing my pain, what else could I do?

Let's say you are in a relationship with someone who "makes" you feel unhappy. The person does not make you feel unhappy. You just don't have shared vision in the relationship. You want one thing and they want another. You want them to behave in a way that would make you feel better or support you somehow. Perhaps your spouse works too much and that makes you feel lonely. From there, it is easy to create a story that says your spouse enjoys work more than spending time with you. It is easy to blame your spouse for making you feel a certain way.

In this case it would be far more productive to understand the story your spouse is telling to him/herself. Can you each adjust your stories to find an outcome that makes you both happy? Sometimes couples will not agree because neither one wants to change their story. What you have is an impasse— however, no one is to blame.

OR, maybe there is a lesson for you. Maybe you need to slow down or give up a friendship. Maybe you need better boundaries with people. Maybe you give too much and people take advantage of your compassionate ear.

NUTRITIONAL THOUGHTS
Do any of these thoughts sound like a good fit for you?

- I do not want to add more pain to someone already in pain.
- I am in control of my life. No one controls me—the best part of being an adult.

- I am grateful for my life. I am sorry that they are not happy.
- If I feel anything negative from this person, I have a choice. I can remove myself. I can breath. I can be compassionate.
- It is smart to remove myself from those who are toxic before I enter into their world of pain.
- I have thousands of choices over my behavior. I cannot make someone else do anything, but I can always choose for myself.
- Is there anything helpful I can do for them?
- After I blame others, I have not changed anything. I am stuck. I hate being stuck.
- I am grateful for my life and I can find ways to improve it.

Can you practice gratitude? Can you see anything in the person you blame for your life circumstances that is wounded? Yes, they are rude or mean, but most negative behaviors come from pain. Can you see their pain?

The situation that you blame for your current pain may be extremely difficult but rehearsing the difficulty does not lead to anything other than more pain. Replace your junk food thought with a nutritional one.

Can you help the person you are blaming for your mood? If so, give them the compassion and understanding they need. Perhaps they are falsely accusing you of something. Tell them your true intention and how the accusation feels. "I truly meant to support you, but I see that was not the outcome. What you are saying about me is hurtful."

Maybe the person you are in a relationship has different goals or is going through a difficult period. This cannot make you feel some way or another. You may not have the same goals or perspective on life. Anyone who has been married more than 10 years has probably experienced a time where you are not feeling aligned. Are you blaming your relationship for keeping you from your goals?

Can you try to understand the other person's perspective? Can you agree to disagree? Maybe your spouse wants to live somewhere you do not want to and you feel stuck. You can always leave. You may not like the options presented, but you are not stuck and it is no one's fault. You are still in control. Make a choice. If you want to stay in the relationship, then you have to decide if this is the compromise you are willing to make. If not, leave.

The idea of gratitude is everywhere now. We hear about journals and daily reminders of gratitude. We all know that we should feel grateful for what we have, especially for those who have a lot. Why is it that, while we understand the concept of gratitude, most of us struggle to remain grateful? Gratitude is a practice. We do not open our eyes and feel a wave of gratitude wash over us. Typically it is just the opposite. We open our eyes and experience stress. Stress of what we have not done; what we need to do; stress over what we are not and where we are not.

Inventory everything that works. Really think about the list.

Rather than blame life for not working the way we hope, attempt to practice gratitude for what works in your life. What is not working is only a reflection of your expectations. Your expectations of where you want to live, work, love, and die are a choice. If you choose to do it another way, you can. Blaming is a waste of time. Make a choice today to live differently or change your expectations.

TAKE ACTION

Find one area that you feel stuck in because someone else's actions are causing a feeling or a situation you do not like. Inventory the choices you do have. Do you hate your boss or job? What choices do you have? You can job search. Maybe you can put in for a transfer to another department. Do you feel stuck in a relationship? You can always leave. You do not have to stay. There are always choices available to you.

After you make a list of choices you can make, rank them from 1-10 in order based on what would make you the happiest. Once they are in order, spend the week taking action into the first and second choice.

Exercising the control you have over your own mindset is very empowering. And as you learn to let go of the things you have no control over, you will quickly see the benefits of your preserved emotional energy. Letting go of the need for blame and the victim mindset feels great!

Emotional Workout #5: Shame

"Shame is the intensely painful feeling or experience of believing that we are flawed and therefore unworthy of love and belonging."
— BRENÉ BROWN

Do you hear yourself saying:

- If I share my true feelings, then others will not love me, want to be friends with me, accept me.
- When I am thinner, richer, have kids, get married, have more success, get into that school, get a promotion, then I will be enough. Anything that indicates that I am not currently good enough, but when I am I can be loved and worthy.
- I am not as interesting as people think, so I am careful about sharing my true feelings.

- I am afraid of rejection.
- I am afraid of getting hurt, so I do not share my thoughts/feelings.
- Others will not love me if they really know me.

Are you silently having thoughts that you need to hide so others don't reject you? Do you make sure you do not get too close to anyone in fear that they will find out the truth about you and leave?

Shame is the most toxic of all the junk food we feed ourselves with because shame tells us that we are wrong at a core level. **The distinction is that we did not do something wrong, we are wrong.** We are born wrong. We are at our essence wrong. The reason it is the most toxic is because if we did not do something wrong, but in fact we are wrong, there is not a whole lot we can do about it. We are damned.

Shame comes in the form of, "I am not enough" or "who do I think I am". In *Daring Greatly*, Brené Brown beautifully explains that we keep ourselves in the cycle of shame because shame thrives when we keep our feelings of unworthiness a secret. As we keep the secret, we cannot heal. Like the person attempting to lose weight—counting calories all day—while secretly eating late at night when no one is watching.

The silence and secrecy of shame keeps us in a cycle that destroys our ability to love and be loved, step forward into our lives fully and feel good about ourselves in the process. While we visualize a perfect world where we will not face rejection or hurt before we move forward, our lives are not waiting for us. **Day after day we wait for perfection to take action.** Because perfection does not exist, we lose our lives to a goal that is impossible to achieve. The joy of telling a loved one how much we love them never happens. The job we covet, but have not worked towards is lost while we prepare and never feel ready.

We work and work to find a perfect moment to step out into our life, but that day does not happen. So we place all our energy into holding back, keeping the secret of our flaws from those closest to us. Holding a space for this self-hatred day in and day out requires so much energy that, if there were no other value from kicking shame, this would be it. The weight that we carry day in and day out that keeps us from enjoying the present moment adds up until our thoughts are consumed with negativity and self hate. The worst part, like the two-packs a day smoker who feels fine, is that we normalize this self-talk and no longer feel its effects.

Have you ever really listened to the awful things you are saying about yourself? What are the sentences of hate that you utter silently and pretend it has no effect. Write down the negative self talk and take one day to say the same sentences to others. Most of us would never speak as badly to others, but feel it is okay to say it to ourselves.

"In your whole life nobody has ever abused you more than you have abused yourself. And the limit of your self-abuse is exactly the limit that you will tolerate from someone else. If someone abuses you a little more than you abuse yourself, you will probably walk away from that person. But if someone abuses you a little less than you abuse yourself, you will probably stay in the relationship and tolerate it endlessly."
— MIGUEL RUIZ, THE FOUR AGREEMENTS

To get in emotional shape, we need to know what we are

working on. Shame denies, lies, avoids and ultimately destroys our ability to make progress. Shame not only tells us that we are flawed, it also tells us that we have to keep our flaws a secret. It tells us that we could lose everything that matters to us if our flaws are known; that we will be rejected in our imperfections. How can we fix something that we will not admit to? How can we improve our emotional health if we deceive ourselves and others of the problem?

Imagine going to a physician with health issues and, when asked where it hurts, pointing to a different part of the body than the one in pain. Or, worse, we don't seek help at all. Sadly, many people do this. The same is true with emotional heath. Relationships are lost forever. Financial troubles become so overwhelming that bankruptcy becomes a last resort. Shame—silence about admitting our flaws—wreaks havoc on our lives destroying our ability to resolve issues by its own nature of silence.

We want to move forward in our lives. We want to make progress. Shame destroys our ability to move forward because we are waiting for the moment that we cannot get hurt or rejected. When we practice self-love, when we love ourselves we cannot get rejected. Someone may not appreciate what we have to offer, but our self-esteem is not contingent on others approvals. We only have control over our self, so we need to control our sense of self. Then we are not at the mercy of the views of others—a place we will never have influence over.

What will happen if you stay in the secrecy and silence? How does it feel in your body to hold that secret? Do you feel it in you chest? Do you have pressure in your eyes? Is your heart heavy? Is the pressure of holding back like an explosion in your chest that you are containing? Does it physically hurt? This feeling will stay for as long as you let it.

How would it feel to release just a little of that pressure? How would you sleep at night without it? Keeping secrets requires work. Letting them free creates space for other parts of your life to grow and expand.

Shame is like the virtual prison where you hold the only key. It is your decision to step out of your cage and reveal yourself in your full humanity. When we hide we accept that we are less than we really are. We allow the shame to take control of our power and potential.

ONE-LINE STRATEGY
Share. We are all flawed. It is better to admit our flaws than to die by them.

EXERCISE

1. Progress is better than perfection.
2. My truth is always worthy because it is mine. Call out the shame thoughts.
3. Be selective. Don't fear showing up because of rejection—the rejecters need to be ejected out of your life.
4. Don't assume hurt or rejection before it happens.
5. Be resilient.
6. Hateful thoughts against myself are as toxic as hateful thoughts against others.
7. Don't judge—just grow.
8. Spend time on life design—what you want, not what others think.
9. Practice self-love.

The shame resilience workout consists of accepting that progress is better than perfection. By locating the junk food thoughts that start your shame cycle and replacing them with nutritional thoughts, you move past the perfection cycle and into your life. Shame keeps us on the life bench waiting for the perfect moment to begin living fully.

No more waiting. Begin today. We are not perfect. No one is. We want to make progress in life, not achieve perfections. Begin by admitting the smallest of flaws that makes you less lovable? Start small. Can you admit to something small? Is there one quality that does not feel as risky to admit? Start there. Write down your favorite shame statements. They lose strength when spoken or written.

Assess what you have written. Is it true? Are you the thing you wrote down? Or is this an imposter voice? Would you ever say this about someone else? Is it mean? What is the fear?

Shame hates to be called out. If you would change jobs, but fear rejection or would step into love or try to love deeper, but fear of getting hurt holds you back, call out the exact words you use.

What if you spoke your truth? What would happen? Would the rejection destroy you? Or are you resilient? Are you strong and resilient? Can you get hurt or rejected and move forward? This person who rejects you—is she really going to or have you made a huge assumption about the person's feelings? Has she rejected you or is this just a general sense you have of people? Locate one friend for a shame share. Share one small shameful fact and notice one thing: you survived. You are resilient. You will not die from sharing your truth.

What do you want? Do you want a deeper relationship? A different job or a change that scares you? This is your truth.

You are entitled to it. Who is in the way? Fear of rejection or judgment holds you back so who is that voice?

It is easy to hide away from the perceived pain you believe you will experience if you step forward. Yes, someone may not value your feelings or may not reciprocate in kind, but you are resilient.

Without all the wasted time hiding what you perceive to be deep internal flaws, you can begin to design the life you desire. This small, but overwhelming thought is standing between you and your dreams. Had I not removed one sentence about what makes a writer and what does not, I would have never written. Imagine what you can achieve, love, and experience if that sense of shame were gone. Imagine if all the energy you used to hide your true self were given back to you, what you could do with that time?

What do you say to yourself when you start your shame cycle?

- I am not that interesting.
- If I speak my truth, I will be rejected.
- I won't be taken seriously.
- No one really cares about me.
- I am not really that good at anything.
- I am not that smart.
- If I tell my real thoughts, I wont be loved.
- If I share my true feelings, I won't be given the respect I need.

Shame lies. Take a moment and ask yourself two simple questions: Is your junk thought true, and what will happen if you move forward and test your assumption?

For example, I thought I did not have a high enough degree to write. Is this true? No, plenty of people write without a higher degree. Secondly, what will happen to me if I move forward and show my work to others? I believed I would get swallowed up alive. As if the person I showed the work to would laugh uncontrollably and I would dissolve in front of their eyes. What did I do? I went right to the source. I showed my parents my writing before anyone else. I went for a marathon run without any warm up.

My assumption was that my work would not meet expectation. I love my parents, but they have really high expectations and I never felt I could meet them. I went into their home, paper in hand and planned for rejection. I don't mean I was ready for a fight, but I had surrendered myself to the outcome. I was ready to take an emotional beat down and not get upset. I was practicing shame resiliency at the source—family.

With my expectations so low and my vulnerability so high, I found myself at peace. It was not the fear of my parents that was so painful to face, but the fear of my own voice. They liked the work and had some negative comments too. But, I was relaxed because I had decided to accept whatever came my way. I removed my assumptions of a negative outcome and without my worst critic, me, I was perfectly fine. Well, that is because I came in with my best workout clothes and kale smoothie. I had a nutritional thought all prepared.

NUTRITIONAL THOUGHTS

- Everyone has some shame.
- Flaws can be attractive. I love people with flaws.

- Love is not contingent on being perfect. "Perfect" people are boring because they are fake.
- I am not bad or good. I am learning and growing. I will learn and grow from this.
- I can be honest with the people I trust.

Shame is exhausting. It takes a lot of work to hold back your truth. Shame slows us down. Shame keeps us from focusing on what matters—our goals and dreams. How can we expect to get anything done? Reframe your junk food thoughts and create a new nutritional perspective:

- I am resilient.
- I am strong.
- I do not avoid negative moments.
- I choose to trust people's intentions.
- I value my life and chose not to waste time on waiting for others to approve.
- Growth is life. I cannot fail, I can only grow.
- I take people at face value and don't assume what they think.
- No one is thinking negative thoughts about me. If they are, they have to go.

My new thought was that I would produce quantity not quality and God would take care of the rest. I let go of perfection in exchange for progress. Progress is better than waiting for perfection. I love my life and my career, even with its imperfections.

SELF-LOVE

How often do you say something kind to yourself?

"I did a good job."

"I was a great friend today."

"I was an amazing parent today."

"I am in great shape."

"I really learned a lot today. I was open and honest."

"I am proud of myself."

If you are like most of us, we shudder at the thought of it. Why? Because we believe we could always do better. I cannot say that I am in good shape because I could always be in better shape. I cannot say that I am a great parent because I could always be a better parent. In other words, I am not enough.

Sure we can always improve, but this misses the core of life. We are here on a journey. There is no final destination of parenting or physical fitness or financial success. There could always be "more." So embrace the idea that there could be more, but celebrate today. Remember we are not after perfection. We are after growth and love. If you were a great parent today, then celebrate that. It can be enough for today. Maybe it is not your ultimate parenting vision, but we want to make progress into the vision, not only celebrate the end goal.

Maybe you are not the best in your line of work, but celebrate the achievements you have made along the way. Self love. A moment of acceptance of what is. Today you are here and loving something, anything about yourself must be possible.

TAKE ACTION

Locate some area you are waiting to step forward in and take one step. Wait. Notice that junk food, the smell, the taste, the texture, and don't take a bite. Remember your new nutritional thought. Think it. Imagine your worst fear and laugh—you will not get eaten alive by other's judgment.

Want to write? Write. Want to draw? Buy a pen. Want to start something? Write a plan. Start with anything. You don't need perfection, just progress. Small and steady.

As you take in your nutritional thoughts, what is the voice saying now? Has it come back with a new message about how much you are an impostor? The craving is strong, but resist the temptation. Imagine how amazing you will feel when you see the truth—you survived and your shame voice exposed, like a label on the container of your favorite processed food, as nothing but junk.

Keep going. Every day the temptation will diminish as you feel better from your new action. The temptation is there and if you cheat a little and eat a bit of junk food thoughts, don't' give up. Come back to your new nutritional habit. Can you step forward every day for a week? Take a moment after each win to celebrate. Yes, you did it and you are free!

"The moment from certainty to uncertainty is what I call fear."
— KRISHNAMURTI, FREEDOM FROM THE UNKNOWN

I removed junk food thoughts from my diet and added supportive nutritional thoughts for months. My craving for junk food thoughts decreased and my appetite for nutritional thoughts grew. My system had worked. I heard the voice telling me, "I needed a higher degree to write a book" and I immediately replaced it with my new thought, "I love books written by people without higher degrees." The faster

I learned to interrupt the thought the faster I interrupted the feeling that came with it; the dread, doubts, anxiety, frustrations slowly faded away. Those unwanted negative emotions were replaced with new emotions: ease, flow, calm, faith, surrender, and joy.

I peeled back layer after layer of junk thoughts filled with self-doubt, fears, assumptions, and I found the very thing that I was looking for: my authentic self. When I started on my quest to find my authentic self I thought the process was going to be simple: ask myself what I really wanted and, *voila*, it would appear. That was not the case. I removed the negative self-talk and found that space I was looking for, but it was nothing like what I had imagined.

I thought my authentic voice was going to speak to me with authority and clarity at all times. What I found was that the authentic voice is less of a strong voice and more of a physical, non-verbal sensation. This sensation is more like an instinct that depends on words to actualize. This is the heart of the challenge I found in locating my authentic voice; that instinct is really easy to drown out when my mind is filled with junk thoughts. Our authentic voice is subtle and deep within; silence and attention to that space is the only way to access its power. When denied the power is diminished and neglected, but when it is honored it possesses the entire universe. Everything you need to know. Everything you need desire, dream, or need is packed densely in this space.

Everything except for one small footnote: fear.

Emotional Workout #6: Fear

As I got in better emotional shape by removing my junk food thoughts and adding in some thoughts that were packed with nutrition to support my goal to leave corporate America to become a writer, I was faced with a problem that I did not see coming: fear.

I thought my fears were coming from my negative thinking—that when I cleared out the negative thoughts, I would be set for life, soaring ahead at full speed forever. In fact, fear is a bit more complicated than I realized.

There are two types of fear: primal gut sense that something is wrong and irrational resistance. Primal fear is important to our survival and can be one of our biggest assets. When we are in trouble, fear can show up and we need to trust it. Someone walking behind us on a dark street and that sense comes up—listen to it. The moment you meet someone and you get a feeling something is not right—listen to it. Those moments can save you from seriously difficult situations.

Then, there is the fear that shows up as we pursue what matters most to us: fear of failure, fear of not being good enough, fear of not being loved back, fear of not being capable enough. This fear is misunderstood as being something we do not want to do. We say, "If I feel this uncomfortable, then I cannot want to do this."

Non-primal fear can feel like mortal danger, except for one difference: dread. If we are not in danger and fear shows up, ask one question: do I feel heavy or light? If you feel heavy then dread has set in and you can trust it is not something to pursue. If you feel fear with a bit of lightness underneath, then proceed!

Have you ever thought about trying something and it feels appealing and horrible all at the same time? Seriously, there is this subtle thing that happens when we cross paths with something that is important to our growth—we feel resistance.

Before I enrolled in what I consider to be Chicago's premier yoga studio, Yogaview, for teacher training, I felt drawn towards it and encountered a wall of resistance against it all at the same time. In other words, I cared. The more I cared, the more resistance appeared because of fear.

Fear. Ever heard what fear stands for? Fuck Everything And Run. I want to run because I care and I could fail. If I fail in an area that I care about, I have to face the possibility that I am not enough.

Imagine something that you are going to do that you do not care about. The feeling is a feeling of heaviness or dread. I may need to get it done, but I do not care deeply about the outcome. Now imagine something that you really want to do. Did fear show up the instant you imagined it? Fear is showing up because you care. You would not have fear if you did not care.

This sensation is life's way of telling us that we are doing exactly the thing we need to do.

There are tasks that we just get done. There are tasks that we dread, but we have to do. There are projects that we dread, but help us reach our greater goals. Then there are the things that we desire and fear. Those are the best ones. When I look back on my life, each time I overcame fear, I found the greatest joy. My clients have goals and fears all at the same time. I know we are on the right track when fear shows up—they care.

We will never overcome fear, but we can learn to live with it.

How to face fear and not run:

1. Acknowledge it is there.
2. Are you in danger? Are you in physical pain? If so, attend to it.
3. If you are safe, remind yourself you are safe.
4. Stop and smile. You are stepping into something important. You care.
5. Focus on the task at hand. Fear wants us to worry about the outcome.
6. Take action. The outcome will become clear later. Small actions are all you have now.
7. Celebrate each small action. You stepped into your truth.

We are born with the primal instinct to feel fear. We fear our parents leaving. Anxiety or dread comes later. Those feelings are when we have to do something we do not want to do. Fear is our friend. It tells us that we are in trouble and it tells us that we are on the path towards our truth. Take a moment to distinguish mortal fear from fear of finding your authentic self—the light within.

"Only the light within us is real. We are not afraid of the dark within ourselves, so much as we are afraid of the light."

— MARIANNE WILLIAMSON

Namaste—*"the divine light in me honors the divine light in you."*

Part Four

Maintaining Your **Emotional Health**

The biggest test of my emotional weight loss came near the end of my writing journey. As a first time writer, getting an agent is not easy. Much like getting funding for a new business, no one wants to bet on an unproven product. This time I was the product and I needed to get an agent to sell my book to a publishing house. Unlike many first time authors, I was able to get the attention of an agent in New York. We quickly made an appointment and I flew to New York to meet for a coffee.

I sat down in my best "I am serious, established, and slightly artsy outfit," ready to sell myself. After years owning a company, this was not hard for me. I had spent years in meetings explaining our company to interested parties. So, I flipped on my sales switch and started talking about Emotional Obesity and the value it has for American Culture. I talked and talked for 10–15 minutes and then awaited a response. Without hesitation, the agent said he loved the idea and wanted to sign with me. There was one caveat: he only wanted to work with me if I was serious about making A LOT of money. If I was not interested in making millions, he was not interested in me.

My first thought was, "Where is the pen?" What else was there to talk about? An agent wanted to work with me and make me rich. Of course, he wanted to see some of my writing. We agreed that I would email him my latest draft and he would send a proposal. As I walked out of that five star hotel, guess what walked right out with me—yep, my imposter voices had kicked in before I even had a chance to tell anyone the good news.

"Sure, he loves the idea, but wait until he reads it. He will see how little you actually know."

"How am I going to see my son when I am famous."

"I should have read the 20 books on my kindle, the ones that I have not finished. Then I might actually know enough about what I'm talking about."

With the thoughts came a wave of nervous anxiety that left me slightly dissociated and fully nauseous. I took a cab back to my hotel as the voices increased and the feelings associated with them grew in equal proportion. By the time the cab hit the front door of my hotel I was a wreck.

Who did I call? The soother of all my emotional havoc: my brother, Brian. And, like always, I started to explain the details with the same vigor as I always had: "There is an agent and he actually loves the idea but he probably won't want to really sign with me when he sees the state of my manuscript. He discussed a book deal, speaking tours, and products. He even talked about a TV show based on the idea. How am I going to deal with all this and be a mother?"

I'd like to report that I got it together in New York, but that would be a lie. I sent the agent my materials and went back to Chicago to await his response. I cannot remember if it was one day or two, but I opened my email and there it was: the proposal. I clicked it open and in incredibly small font were the line-by-line details about everything we discussed. He still loved the idea.

I read the proposal once, but I am not sure I paid attention to anything it said. I was so distracted by the simple fact that he did not hate what I sent him. I reread the document and soon a sinking, heavy feeling started to replace the high I was on as I saw: *get a co-author, sell products on QVC, do a speaking series*. These are all good options, so what was with this deep sense of dread? What was this horrible feeling? I called my family and friends to discuss the details. Everyone expressed joy and happiness for my seemingly obvious winning moment. So, why was it that as I was talking about this opportunity, I simultaneously felt like my pet just died?

It was my authentic self.

It was talking to me, but I was not listening. I was so caught up in the moment and the external facts, that I was ignoring my true voice. I got off the phone. I stopped weighing out the pros and cons. I quieted my mind and honored this sense. Was this my true self? Why is it telling me to stop? Who passes on an agent? Apparently, I do.

It was my turning point. I knew I did not want to approach my book in the same way that this agent did. I knew I had to honor that desire; that I had to honor myself. And, I did. I went against all logic and all of my pro and con lists and I listened to myself. I wrote the agent and told him that I did not want to move in the same direction he did. I read and reread my email and, in a moment of true dedication to my new path towards authenticity, performed the most violent act my ego had ever suffered. I hit send and off my email went.

It was one of the most emotionally fit moments of my life.

What is the value of emotional workouts? I don't get to show off my six-pack or walk into a room, rocking the latest trend in a size 6. And while flexing strong muscles feels good, emotional fitness is far better than the feeling I get from physical fitness. In fact, the more emotionally fit I became—and the more I prioritized my own wellbeing—the easier physical fitness got too. I felt lighter. I felt in control. To put it simply, I felt great.

Like every exercise, the more I practiced prioritizing my emotional health the better I became at it and the better I felt.

The meeting request that did not work in my schedule was denied; the negative feedback loops were replaced with more empowering thoughts. Obligations became questions about what I wanted to do, not just what I believed was expected from me. Negative moments came, but they didn't take such a strong hold of my senses. I could let go. I could move forward, free of the emotional weight that wanted to drag me down. Most importantly, I applied this to every component of my life and felt the benefits of my emotional sweating, sore muscles and stretching.

Emotional weight makes us feel tired, unhappy, and sluggish as our junk thoughts create chaos and weigh us down. Emotional fitness gives us energy and supports us to achieve our dreams. Our spirit, soul, and authentic self must manifest though our physical bodies. It depends on our minds to use language to become stronger, louder, and clearer. So, while emotional fitness may not give us abs of steel, we get to jump out of bed into a life that we truly love with the energy of our unburdened self. **Our days are filled with hard work, but the hard work is also uplifting and energizing**. Because when you do what your authentic self desires hard work becomes both work and a source of energy.

But how do we maintain that energy? Let's be honest, if it were not for the occasional bikini moment, we would all probably pack on an extra few pounds. But summer is an excellent threat/motivation to maintain our physical shape. So how do we find motivation to maintain our emotional fitness?

Once we shed the weight of some old emotional baggage, we will just need to maintain a healthy emotional lifestyle. Unless there is a major life event—which may require a little extra help—it just becomes an exercise of daily discipline. It is not chaotic or overwhelming and totally worth doing.

The key is to tie our desire for change with a reason that is motivating to us. Then the odds of success are much higher. Finding what really motivates you will increase your ability for success. Are you making the change for your children? Are you making it for your spouse? Are you making it for yourself? Identify your purpose and let it guide your practice.

They call yoga a practice because it is something that has to be done regularly to get the benefits from it. Coming from my authentic self was something I had to practice. I had to practice fearlessness and courage. I had to practice trusting in my truth. I had to have faith that it was okay to follow my truth and that the universe would show me the path. I had to practice showing vulnerability to allow my voice a space to shine. I had to learn about self-compassion.

When I began, I would deny myself all the positive messages that I would happily say to a friend. All the dreams I would take pleasure in helping manifest for someone else, I would not allow for myself. All the values I would say mattered in life, I would not live by. I was able to turn this around by discovering my true motivation and it became a single message that I habitually told myself: I am my son's teacher.

Influence

"The only true wisdom is in knowing you know nothing."

— PLATO

Why would Plato state that wisdom comes from knowing nothing? Isn't it the other way around? Knowledge and education are how we attain real wisdom, right? Nope. Knowledge is critical to function in the world, but wisdom comes from understanding that we never "know" anything because life never stops evolving.

True growth happens in the presence of letting go of the belief that we know it all. Our lives never stop moving and changing. We have to change with it to avoid unnecessary pain. Allowing for each moment to be new, filled with possibility, is essential for happiness. We also have to understand and accept our own power to influence ourselves and those we love. How we use that influence is a choice: Do we try to be "right" all the time, or do we use it to encourage growth and learning?

One of my most powerful motivators is the influence I have over my son. It was a difficult realization at first—to comprehend how the choices and actions I made could affect his emotional wellbeing. Especially when I felt I messed up.

I loved sports as a child so I placed my six-year old son on the soccer team. He was very clear with me that he did not like it, but because I valued soccer and sports, I ignored his comments and campaigned for soccer by touting all the benefits and joys he could experience. *"You'll have a great time. You'll see!"* As his mother, I felt like I needed to expose him to things because, without trying, how would he know what he liked? Over the next two years I made inroads into his view of the sport. He showed some level of happiness playing soccer—or so I thought. Every day he complained about going and every day he would have some fun when he got there. I took that to mean we were on the right track.

But after two years of practices and Saturday games, I came to realize the experiment was just *my campaign*. I finally asked myself, *"Is it possible that my son is wrong? That he doesn't understand his own likes and dislikes?"* I knew the answer was no. And I knew my actions were telling him the opposite. My influence was teaching my son to set aside his true feelings for the sake of pleasing someone else. I surrendered and simply asked him what he wanted to do. Thankfully, he still had his own values intact and said he wanted to quit. I honored his feelings.

We tried guitar at his request and I have not heard a complaint yet. Is my son an artist and not an athlete? It's possible. What would have happened if I had continued pushing an identity on him that did not fit? What if he was successful at soccer and woke up in 20 years in a world that he never enjoyed but because of external praise from family and society he continued down a path he didn't want? He could leave home and "move on" with his life, but his life would not of his making. His life would have been designed by the joys and views of others. The worst part is that he would never know. The memory and understanding of how he ended up with sports instead of music would be a thing of the past. However there would be one lingering element: he would never know the passion and joy that would otherwise be possible. My son could experience success, but not joy. **We cannot experience true joy when we live a life meant for someone else.**

When our life's teachers match our spirit, then this is not an issue. But, what about when we have different needs and views than the parents, mentors, teachers who designed our life's lens?

"THE WAY I AM" ISN'T THE WAY YOU HAVE TO BE

Even in our day-to-day lives, the voices of those who influenced us can dictate our choices and actions. I had a father who never turned away from a good fight. I do the same. Something said in a fight triggers a voice that says, "I should stand up for myself," demanding that I hold my own in an argument. Yes, my father and I have similar temperaments, but I adopted his beliefs and never looked back.

I don't believe in fighting every fight. When I finally recognized that this principle was not in line with my beliefs. I went on a mission to break the unhealthy emotional pattern I had been following and stopped arguing with people as much. Now, I am raising my son with a different philosophy. This is not about right and wrong, it is about designing life to mirror the person you are and will always be—not the person you learned to be.

HABIT

We all know if we do not exercise for ten years and then go out and run a marathon, we will be in a lot of pain. So, if we accept this to be true of physical fitness, then why would we expect anything different for emotional fitness? No one wants to work out every day. No one wants to eat healthy all the time because it is just easier to eat whatever we want and watch TV. But if we want to be in shape, it takes work, discipline, and habit.

Emotional health requires both awareness and good habits. My clients become aware of their particular draw to certain junk thoughts quickly, but awareness alone will not get them the emotionally fit results they desire. Once they are aware of the thoughts, they need to practice replacing them with nutritional thoughts that support their true desires.

NLP teaches that saying incantations out loud is the quickest way to create a new habit. Repeating your nutritional thoughts out loud while in action—say them in the car, jogging, walking, cleaning the house, anywhere—will quickly assimilate them into your consciousness. Equally, repeating your junk thoughts out loud in a less than serious voice is a highly effective way to diffuse them. Our brains hear what we say. It does not know what is happening without our senses feeding it information. In other words, if you tell your brain something is terrible, it will believe you. Your authentic self is smarter and will reject persuasion toward a direction it does not want to go. The brain doesn't know the difference. So, use that to your advantage. Repeat the negative junk thoughts in as goofy a voice as you can muster up. If you have ever inhaled the helium from a balloon, then you have a perfect silly voice example. Nothing can be taken seriously from that place.

Over time the junk thoughts quiet and loosen their grip over your feelings and then over your actions. The nutritional thoughts will get stronger and stronger until they are the dominant, go-to emotional muscle. Once this occurs, the heavy lifting is not needed to keep them in place.

My tendency towards thoughts of inadequacy still arises in difficult moments. In fact, each time I hand my newest writing to my editor, or each time I send out my manuscript for a read, I hear that voice telling me how much they will be disappointed in my output of ideas. Fortunately, I have built the emotional habits to counteract these negative feelings. Now, with my new emotional muscles, I just reach for a 5-pound weight and start my reps: "They are entitled to their opinion." "Maybe they will have something helpful to tell me so I can make the best book possible." "I have done my best and I am proud that I completed the work."

Once I successfully set a foundation of thoughts down that mirrored my true beliefs, I was able to take actions in accordance with those foundational thoughts.

The Importance of Action

Isolating the area you want to change but then never taking action toward it is like dreaming of a better body while watching TV. If you do not get up and work out, you will not lose a pound. **Having an honest, authentic feeling or moment of self-awareness is not enough. Action must be taken from that space, from that thought.** Take one action toward your new goal. Any action. The more you can actually do in a day the better. It is one of the most important habits you can develop.

Every time I think about working out, I have a bunch of voices telling me to stay in bed or that I will do it tomorrow. Or, I do not have time. The dividing line is that I know that those are excuses and I have to get up and do yoga or go to the gym or I will not get in shape. The same is true with emotional fitness. I may tell myself that I cannot do something for a million reasons, but that does not mean I have to listen. Focusing on the goal of getting in shape because of a wedding in a month, or because summer is coming and bathing suit season is around the corner, all help the commitment to get up and go to the gym. Replacing the thoughts of our warm bed with the goal and belief that we want to get in shape will help us take action.

"You can only be afraid of what you think you know."
— JIDDU KRISHNAMURTI

Taking the action necessary to move in a new direction—to pull our bodies out of that warm bed—requires fearlessness. I was putting myself in a new situation that would require me to trust in a new path. It was scary. I was afraid. Often this fear is enough to quit. We want to know where our actions will lead and that we will be okay. My fear disappeared once I started trusting my authentic voice to lead my life's direction. As Krishnamurti says, my mind was capable of creating and responding to scenarios that were far more terrifying than they needed to be. When I let go of my preconceived notions and expectations—when I allowed myself to move forward *without knowing what would happen*—I was calmer and more at peace.

Faith

Sooner or later, emotional fitness becomes a journey into the spiritual. When we say we do not like change and we do not like doing differently it is because we do not know the outcome. We like to stay where we are, even if we are suffering because it is familiar. What are we saying? We are saying that changing our circumstance is uncomfortable because it leads us away from what we know. What I know now is that I don't know much.

There is a measure of faith that must come with emotional fitness because we have to trust that we are always okay despite the shifting of our external world. We cannot push our will on the universe and try to bend the current situation to match our needs. We have to trust that we can make changes and the universe will be there to catch us. **Fearlessness is the secret ingredient to emotional fitness because it allows us to have the courage to show up in our life as we were meant to be.** Free from the misguided messages of family and culture. Fearless to show up with all our truths and vulnerabilities is a spiritual act. It is spiritual because we are acting from our spirit, our true self.

My spiritual path was a slow one filled with set backs and detours. Because of my upbringing I had so many layers of learned beliefs that I had to peel back to find my authentic self. As I found this mysterious place, I had to practice and practice returning to it for guidance because my emotional habits were so based on the belief that my mind would guide me to the "right" answer as long as I used logic to arrive there. Logic is an interesting thing.

As a student of philosophy, I was fascinated to learn that people *created* logic as a system to come to an answer. In all my years of study, I never understood why it was accepted as a system that came to real truths. Socrates, the godfather of logic, clearly explains that we will never know anything as it really exists. In fact, he states that true wisdom is the acceptance that we will never know anything in this world: "The only true wisdom is in knowing you know nothing."

Our only truth is the truth that is within.

For years I took that to mean the truth is mine and therefore I am separate from others. Nothing could be further from reality. For years I struggled to peel back layer after layer of beliefs that I was an individual and that I could not see the world any other way. Slowly, as I became more emotionally fit, I realized the opposite was true. "You are the universe, expressing itself as a human for a little while," says Eckhart Tolle. I am the universe and it is using my body this time to express its truths. I am not here for any other reason than to communicate its truths through my actions. This realization changed my perspective.

I practiced fearlessness: fearless to act against culture;

fearless to act against family; fearless to act against logic; fearless to act against my own misguided beliefs that felt so real; fearless to walk the path I wanted to walk.

> *You say I am repeating*
> *Something I have said before. I shall say it again.*
> *Shall I say it again? In order to arrive there,*
> *To arrive where you are, to get from where you are not,*
> *You must go by a way wherein there is no ecstasy.*
> *In order to arrive at what you do not know*
> *You must go by a way which is the way of ignorance.*
> *In order to possess what you do not possess*
> *You must go by the way of dispossession.*
> *In order to arrive at what you are not*
> *You must go through the way in which you are not.*
> *And what you do not know is the only thing you know*
> *And what you own is what you do not own*
> *And where you are is where you are not.*
>
> — T.S. ELIOT

Each and every time I thought about what to do in my life I learned to turn inward and seek the truth within. This space was not always popular with those around me or, to be honest, it was not popular with me. I had to have fearlessness to step forward anyway. I had to have faith that this space existed and that it would be my guide.

I practiced having faith in something that is invisible, voiceless, and cannot be measured. For some it happens in a moment, for me it happened over years. Whatever road I took to get here, I am grateful.

Once I understood the simplicity of faith, my life filled with ease, joy and peace. The external world continues to move and push into me, but now, with my new emotional exercises, I am prepared to keep up with the endless gravitational pull that we are all part of—the one that pulls us towards what does not serve us. As I find myself moving towards the emotional cake, chips, or cigarettes, I stop. I come back to that deep sense and wait for the guidance I need to proceed forward in the right direction. **Despite my ego fighting this guidance, I follow its endless wisdom.**

We want to make the "right" choice. We want to choose the popular road. We want to make others happy. We want to contribute to the world. The mistake is to trust the messages we have received from outside us to get there. **The true choice will originate from our unique creative voice manifesting the singular truth of the world.**

The Wave

I stopped trusting my voices of judgment and ideas of right and wrong and began to trust that what was being offered to me was exactly what I was manifesting. If I were open and connecting to abundance and joy, then the universe would shower me with abundance.

However, when we get in shape emotionally we have to learn to come back to ourselves, our spirit. To do this we have to learn how to find it again.

This is done though a process of surrendering and letting go, of not pushing into our new goal. Surrender was a word that I had never considered. Surrender had always meant giving up or quitting. In fact, the definition of surrender is to give up control. Why would anyone want to give up control and surrender into anything?

Working hard toward something is not always productive. In this case, the idea is to surrender and give up control because the thought pattern is not working. To surrender, to give up control, creates space. From this space the universe is able to show you another path.

Everything I ever needed to learn about change, I learned from handstand. I had always been reasonably athletic, but the idea of going upside down at 35 and trusting that my arms would support me, sounded like one of the worst ideas ever. I didn't want to do it. *At all.* Unfortunately, most yoga classes I attended included a 5-minute phase during which we would go to the wall to practice handstands. To say that fear was the dominant feeling I possessed, was an understatement. I would place my hands on the floor and think, "This is impossible."

However, since the room was filled with women my age flipping up into handstands, my ego would get the best of me and I would fling my body against the wall with aggression and a total lack of grace. Each class would be a repetition of the last and my growing hatred of handstands became palpable. One afternoon, the teacher brought up handstands again and I dragged myself to the wall, sat on my heels and stared blankly. Then, I committed a yoga faux pas and looked over at another student. She was also struggling with handstand, but in a totally different way. She would attempt to kick up, work hard, and then close her eyes and rest until she was calm and ready to try again. I sat there, dripping sweat, mesmerized by her focus and surrender to the action.

Well, I thought, *why not give that a try?*—It certainly looked better than what I was doing. I closed my eyes, settled my mind and, when I was without judgment or expectation, I placed my hands down on the floor and kicked towards handstand. I still did not get up all the way and, believe it or not, I did not care. I actually just gave up caring about the outcome and embraced the process from this place of calm, compassion for myself. I accepted the challenge, knowing that was hard for me.

Months went by and each day I kicked and kicked with no attachment to the outcome. I would stop—just like the woman I had seen—rest, come back to a calm place, and then try again. One day, I went over to the wall again to attempt my handstand and—without thought or intention—I kicked up, still, calm and content. Well, until I noticed that I had gotten into a handstand and started to celebrate, which immediately caused me to fall.

The reason that this was so powerful is because when we approach life without the voice of judgment and fear, sit quietly and create a space for ourselves to try something new, surrendering our expectations, it can become effortless. I had surrendered my control over the handstand and allowed my body to do what it naturally could or not could not do.

We are so bogged down with thoughts of fear that we are not working and trying to do the things we want in life. When I let go of all attachment to the outcome and the process, I learned to kick into handstand. When I let go of all attachment to the outcome of my job, I was able to write this book. When we let go and allow the natural flow of life to move us through our days, life leads us on a journey; we have control but we also learn to receive what comes our way. **Trying too hard to enforce our will on the universe only limits our options.**

The illusion of achievements and goals closes us off to the opportunities that exist. Sitting back and allowing the universe to show us the path instead of imposing our hopes on the universe opens up opportunities. We will still have to work hard, but there will be ease in the work. When we are aligned with our inner self, life moves naturally and work requires less effort, not more.

Emotional workouts are more about letting go and stepping back than pushing forward.

In my journey from emotional obesity towards emotional fitness, I found that the more fit I became the more life began to happen in front of me. In other words, I found that getting in shape emotionally looked like someone surfing. A surfer paddles out in the ocean and looks around for a wave that feels good to them, without knowing the true nature of the wave. Once they have found the wave that feels right they swim ferociously towards it, jump on the board and ride the wave in whichever way the sea offers. The surfer may have picked a wave that rides them into the shore or one that breaks, dropping them in the water to try again.

Once I shed emotional weight and learned to recognize my imposter voices, the "sea" became a happier environment. I found that if I paddled around, waiting for an opportunity that felt good to me, and jumped in even if I didn't know whether it would ride me to shore or drop me in the sea, everything else happened as it should. If the wave was smaller and did not get me to shore, I would paddle back out, wait, look for the one that felt right for me and then hop back on again. Some times the wave would bring me to the shore and sometimes it would not, but I always rode the wave.

Surfers know they cannot guide the waves. They learn how to ride, they practice their moves and balance, and then they trust themselves and the sea. I've learned that the wave will determine how far I will go, assuming I hold on for the ride. Now, I do not care about the size of the wave or the path it will take. I just pick the one that feels best and I surrender to the power of the universe. **I accept that in the moment that the wave and I meet the wave will be in control, not me.** And that is okay. I can always catch another one and I can always just paddle around.

When I was able to silence the negative messages of my imposter voices then I was able to choose my wave from my true heart's desire. In those moments, I did not worry about how far the ride to shore would be. I did not worry if I picked the wrong wave. I did not worry if I could handle the next twist or turn because I was just focused on standing on my board, watching where the wave was leading me. Every time I thought an opportunity was not right, it was because I assumed I was able to predict the destination of that path.

Yes, one wants to give thought to the path they take, but ultimately your true self—your heart's decision—has to pick the wave or opportunity and then surrender all control. Work hard to stay on your board, focus on the twists and turns because it is there you will have to be able to respond, but the outcome of the wave's destination is unknown. Have faith and surrender to the belief that the wave knows how to be a wave. The wave, this world, and the universe in all its mystery cannot be controlled by our will.

Conclusion

The only truth is the truth of the self that comes from within. This space is endlessly wise, but hard to find amongst the noise of the mind. We are here and we are safe because our spirit is never concerned with what changes in the external world. It is okay to change jobs, relationships, cities, or our outlook because we are not changing anything that matters. What matters most is that the changes we make are created from the voice of our spirit. Changes in that direction will always create a sense of safety, a sense of being in the flow of life. Changes away from our spirit will create a sense of fear and pain.

Emotional obesity, lacking awareness of what we think, not taking responsibility for our thoughts and not taking action from our true beliefs places a barrier between our soul and us. The pain that we experience is the pain of moving away from our self, away from our spirit, away from God. When we can own our thoughts, make decisions from our soul, we are coming back to the divine from which we are created. As Sutra 2.16 teaches us, *"Pain that has not yet come is* avoidable." Joy, freedom, self-expression, love, gratitude, all come from the choice to wake up to the negative messages we tell ourselves, take control of our thoughts and turn towards the divine light that shines in us all.

> Except for the point, the still point,
> There would be no dance, and there is only the dance.
> I can only say, there we have been: but I cannot say where.
> And I cannot say, how long, for that is to place it in time.
> The inner freedom from the practical desire,
> The release from action and suffering, release from the inner
> And the outer compulsion, yet surrounded
> By a grace of sense, a white light still and moving...
>
> — T.S. ELIOT, FOUR QUARTETS

Made in United States
Troutdale, OR
07/27/2023

11602760R00118